WEIRDNESS, WEIRDNESS EVERYWHERE

MEDICAL MILESTONES
Boston Celtics broadcaster Johnny Most went to the doctor for an examination to see why he was having trouble hearing. The doctor checked his ear and found a radio ear plug, which had been in Most's ear for eighteen months.

ALL IN THE FAMILY
A Tacoma, Washington, woman received thirty days in jail for keeping her 8-year-old stepgrandson in a box for two years. She let him out only to use the bathroom and attend church. The boy told his rescuers he was surprised to learn that all little boys aren't kept in boxes.

OOPS
The West Virginia highway department built a two-lane bridge for a three-lane section of the state turnpike. Department spokesman John Gallagher blamed designers for the error, which officials didn't notice until the bridge was actually built. "It sounds a lot worse than it is," Gallagher added.

UNUSUAL WEAPONS
In 1978, a Paris grocer stabbed his wife to death with a wedge of Parmesan cheese.

CHUCK SHEPHERD teaches law and regulation at the George Washington University business school and writes the weekly "News of the Weird" feature, which appears in several dozen daily and weekly newspapers. JOHN J. KOHUT is a political analyst for a large corporation in Washington, D.C. ROLAND SWEET is a magazine editor and a regular contributor of weird news to several alternative newspapers.

NEWS OF THE
WEIRD

Chuck Shepherd
John J. Kohut
Roland Sweet

Illustrations by Drew Friedman

A PLUME BOOK

REGISTERED TRADEMARK—MARCA REGISTRADA

Library of Congress Cataloging-in-publication Data

Shepherd, Chuck.
  News of the weird / by Chuck Shepherd, John J. Kohut, and Roland Sweet.
    p.   cm.
  ISBN 0-452-2611-5
  1. Curiosities and wonders—United States—Anecdotes. 2. United States—History,
Local—Anecdotes. I. Kohut John J. II. Sweet, Roland. III. Title.
E179.S549   1989
973—dc20   89-12392
                                                                        CIP

First Printing, November, 1989

      3   4   5   6   7   8   9

PRINTED IN THE UNITED STATES OF AMERICA

Acknowledgments

Many, many people have helped the authors over the last fifteen years.

Jim White, Jamie Moore, Bill Harris, Joe Kohut, Magdalen Kohut, Peter Favini, Susan Scheer, Melissa Walker, and Jake Geesing.

And then there are Mike Greenstein, Steve Moss, Alan Stamm, John Kokot, Richard Jahnke, Bob LaRussa, Pat Steer, Tom Peyer, John Duffie, Rick Mariani, Kihm Winship, Bill Lawitts, Charles Fort, Norbert Pearlroth, H. Allen Smith, George Ives, Theodora Tiffany Tilton II, and Olfa.

And we'd like to pay homage to the "competition" (whom we fawningly admire)—John Bendel and his predecessors responsible for turning out "True Facts" in *National Lampoon* nearly every month for 17 years.

And, of course, there are Ed Aderer, Brian Allred, Linda Anderson, Lee Arbetman, Irwin Arieff, Brian Armstrong, Tom Arnold, Russell Ash, Peter Aspesi, J. M. Barker, Richard Beck, Steven Bennett, Michael Bergman, Jack Beyer, Patrick Bishop, Faxon Bishop, Randall Bloomquist, Randle Brashear, Dan Brennan, T. S. Child, Ed Cohen, Paul Comeau, Helen Cordes, Ron Cotterill, Gaal Shepherd Crowl, John Cunningham, Linda Cunningham, Gene Curry, Kurt Darr, Henrietta Davis, Nancy Debevoise, Whit Deschner, Ed Dolnick, Craig D'Ooge, Tim Dorr, Martha Duggan, Mike Dunn, Ernie Englander, Margaret Engle, David Enna, Paul Evans, Bob Falfa, Korrine Fitz, Dan Free, Sam Gaines, Chuck Gardner, Gerald George, Jonathan Ginsburg, Gail Gleeson, Bill Golden, Leslie Goodman-Malamuth, Joe Goulden, Alan Green, Eric Haines, C. J. Hall, Libby Hatch,

Ellen Haug, Bill Healy, Eric Helwig, Alison Hess, Alex Hooke, Dave Hotaling, Dorothy John, Bob Jones, Chuck Jones, John F. Jones, Jim Kane, Fred Kanter, Rich Kline, Jane Kochersperger, Paul Krassner, Ross Laroe, Bruce Larsen, Sylvia Lee, J. Michael Lenninger, Ray Lesser, Michael Lewyn, Myra Linden, Fred Lipton, Everett Long, Dale Lowdermilk, Michael Lubin, James MacDougall, Ross MacKenzie, Leonard Magargee, Steve Magnuson, Paul Maiorana, Johnny Marr, Melissa Matusevich, Fred McChesney, Gary McGinty, Peter Michaels, Chuck Miller, Justin Mitchell, Joe Mooney, Carol Moore, John Morgan, Jim Mullin, Kenneth Nahigian, Tom Nelson, John Odgers, Scott Parker, Jenny Parks, Matt Paust, John Pell, Matt Perry, Hilary Pfeifer, Linda Phillips, Lee Plave, Yvonne Pover, Rollo Rayjaway, Barbara Kate Repa, Ricky Richardson, Michael Robinson, Daniel Rosenberg, Gail Ross, Jay Russell, Stan Saplin, Jack Shafer, Susan Shaughnessy, Georgene Slagle, Asa Sparks, Allan Spitzer, Lou Stein, Debby Stirling, Jim Sweeney, Tony Tellier, Brian Thompson, Lang Thompson, Bill Triplett, Champ Tunno, Marty Turnauer, Eric Utne, John Vogl, Mike Vogl, Kevin Walsh, Kasey Warner, Bill Wauters, Debbie Weeter, Tracy Westen, Sparky Whitcomb, Don Williams, Elliott Woodward, and Susan Zurcher.

And especially Kenneth Anger, Stephanie Clipper, Gene Grealish, Bob Maslow, Ray Nelke, Chip Rogers, and Elaine Weiss.

Contents

Introduction 1

Get-Poor-Quick Schemes 4

All in the Family 7

Smooth Reactions 11

Animal Tales 14

Weird Punishment 17

The Honeymoon's Over 20

Medical Milestones 23

Penis Envy 28

Handicapable 31

Litigious Society 34

Gunplay 38

Oops 42

Insolent Chariots 47

Celebrity Corner 50

Occupational Hazards 53

Odd Ends 56

Sex Is Its Own Punishment 62

Injudicious Judges 65

Weird Undertaker Stories 69

Jealous Rages 71

Weird Clergy 74

Unusual Weapons 77

Weirdos in Training 79
Weird Pieces of Legislation 83
Products of Free Enterprise 86
Spectacular Suicide Attempts 90
From the Police Blotter 94
Weird TV and Radio 101
Least Justifiable Homicides 103
Inappropriate Uses for Food 105
Least Competent Criminals 108
Wrong Place at the Wrong Time 112
Reasons Not to Dial 911 116
Famous Collectors 119
Memorable Joyrides 122
Mistaken Identities 125
They Still Do That? 127
Feuds 130
Contests 132
Fetishes 134
Compulsive Behavior 136
Nude Behavior 139
Most Compelling Explanations 142
Happenings in the Home 145
Government in Action 148
Unexplained Phenomena 151
Uncategorically Weird 154
Sources 159

Introduction

The perception is that truth is stranger than fiction; in reality, true stories are often stranger than fiction writers can even *imagine.*

The three of us collect true stories with both an evangelist's fervor and a surgeon's diligence. Roland Sweet has been at it since the early 1970s, when he lived in Syracuse, first motivated by the realization that most people don't die dignified deaths and that some people were swapping their babies for cars, appliances, drugs, and beer. Chuck Shepherd began his collection in the mid 1970s, partly as a response to the *ennui* of the eight Nixon-Ford years (and no wonder "News of the Weird" is peaking now, after eight Reagan years!). John Kohut started saving bizarre news stories as an adjunct to graduate study in political science at Chapel Hill, N. C., around 1978.

Roland shares his in the "News and Blues" column of the weekly *Syracuse New Times*, where he served as editor and then, after leaving Syracuse, as contributing editor. Chuck and John shared their items in newsletters, photocopied and circulated at their own expense. Chuck's is *View from the Ledge*, a four-pager begun in 1981 and now in its 28th edition. John's is the massive *The Caretakers of Earth*, now in its 13th edition. While John kept his circulation list to manageable proportions of friends, Chuck circulated *View* widely, with the result that he found many other people who collect weird news, which they were willing to share with him in exchange for staying on the mailing list for *View*. (Over 2,000 people have received *View* at one time or other; the regular list now is around 400; and maybe two dozen are serious collectors the authors view as peers.)

John has the most eclectic interests of the three, ranging from ordinary craziness to strange science and the paranormal. He is fascinated, for example, with the man in Pennsylvania who runs what is best described as "Bigfoot Central": Every news story of Bigfoot activity in the Pennsylvania-Ohio-New York region inevitably contains a comment from this guy, giving perspective to the current sighting. But John is equally interested in the "exploding head syndrome," inconsistencies in science reporting of outer space, and the psychology of the need to joyride.

Roland, as a professional journalist, is a ravenous digester of all news (but the only news that seems to have an impact on him is the strange stuff). He seeks it energetically from out-of-the-way sources such as R. Emmett Tyrrell's column in *The American Spectator*; trade magazines like *Pizza Today*; the flagships of daily reporting of weird news—The *San Francisco Chronicle* and *The Miami Herald*; and emerging new sources, such as the atheist's bible, *Freethought Today*.

Chuck's work recently has consisted of merely reading his mail. The bulk of his collection comes from correspondents who clip their local papers in exchange for *View from the Ledge*. His favorites are stories about the legal system, business, and politics, but he is also the only one of us who keeps up with the supermarket tabloids (even though none of their stories makes it into this book or any of our publications). Chuck's weekly column, "News of the Weird" (distributed by Universal Press Syndicate), appears in newspapers in Los Angeles, San Francisco, Detroit, Denver, Miami, Philadelphia, Washington, D.C., and several dozen other cities.

Why do you and we find this stuff so interesting? For us, maybe it's because we each share a sense of rage against "the usual" in society; we experience vicariously the unconventional behavior, reported every day, of ordinary people who have temporarily broken free of the mainstream. In almost every case, we couldn't have imagined this kind of behavior actually to have taken place—until we read it.

Here are over 500 news stories that we had to read to imagine. Many of them struck us as funny; some we regarded as scary; some aroused pity; some left us speechless. All of them are weird.

Between the three of us, we've got several thousand more weird news items, but these are, to us, the most remarkable stories of the last 15 years. Perhaps you'll agree with our judgment. Perhaps you'll believe that some are too disgusting. Perhaps you might think some news that *you've* saved is even more remarkable. Whatever your reaction, we'd love to hear from you because, unlike "professional writers" who turn out books like this, the three of us live, breathe, eat and sleep weird news—and respect it with almost religious deference. Write us at Strange News, P.O. Box 25682, Washington, D.C. 20007.

Before you start reading, keep a couple of things in mind. Every item has been reported in a mainstream news source and has not, to the best of our knowledge, been withdrawn or repudiated or proven false or misleading. ("Mainstream" news source includes *The New York Times, The Washington Post, Los Angeles Times, The Wall Street Journal, The Miami Herald, San Francisco Chronicle, The Philadelphia Inquirer*, and many other daily newspapers in the U.S. and overseas and general-circulation magazines, as well as Associated Press, United Press International, and Reuters wire reports.) However, we have only collected the items; we have not investigated any independently. Consequently, if the wire service reporter erred in the original news report, the error might be here, also.

And now, enjoy! Try to get neither too amused nor too depressed, and let us know what you think.

Chuck Shepherd
John J. Kohut
Roland Sweet

Get-Poor-Quick Schemes

In Baton Rouge, Louisiana, a man was sentenced to five years' probation for trying to pass a counterfeit $20 bill that he had made by cutting the corners off a real $20 bill and pasting them on a $1 bill. Federal Judge John Parker called him "the most inept counterfeiter I ever heard of."

◼

A New York City woman paid two men $20,000 to beat her husband to death with a baseball bat. He survived. She paid the men $150,000 to shoot him. He took six bullets but survived. Then the hit men charged her $300,000 for another try, promising this time to get it right. The police arrested all three.

◼

A South Korean police officer took a $6 bribe from a motorist, but found himself blackmailed by two men, including a fellow police officer who saw the bribe. The officer paid them $28,750 not to report him, but his superiors found out anyway and demoted him.

◼

Police in Wichita, Kansas, arrested a 22-year-old man at an airport hotel after he tried to pass two counterfeit $16 bills.

The Virginia lottery lets the state collect back taxes and other bills from winners. A woman with a $1,000 winning ticket had a $200 debt, so she gave the ticket to a man to cash for her. The man obliged but forgot he had an $800 debt himself and collected only $200.

When a man presented a $789 income tax refund check to Houston pawnbroker Ted Kipperman, the man also produced an identification card giving his name as "Ernestine and Robert Hayes," just as it appeared on the check. Kipperman said the man explained his mother had been expecting twins and when they didn't show up she gave him both names.

A 21-year-old man who robbed a convenience store in Portland, Oregon, fled with the money but left the keys to his getaway van on the counter. When he returned to the store and demanded his keys, the clerk refused and told him the police were on their way. They arrived in time to arrest him.

In Buffalo, New York, a 24-year-old man was arrested for trying to sell marijuana—inside police headquarters. Patricia Bowers, a report technician, said a man poked his head inside her office doorway. "I said, 'Can I help you, sir?' " Bowers explained. "He said, 'Yeah, do you want to buy some reefer?' "

Bowers summoned narcotics detective Joseph Riga, who was wearing street clothes. Riga said the man then offered to sell him a bag of marijuana for $5. "I thought he was joking at first," Riga said. "Then he pulled out a bag of pot."

The Colorado Court of Appeals upheld the conviction of a man who claimed his constitutional rights were violated when police laughed at him for stealing 1,200 animal rectums. The two police officers who arrested the man and a companion outside a meat warehouse found several boxes of meat in their car, then summoned the warehouse manager, who confirmed his firm had processed the contents—inedible rectal tissue, known as rennets, which are used to cure cheese.

While driving to jail, one of the arresting officers began laughing and told the man what he had stolen. The suspect replied, "If I go to jail for stealing 1,200 [rennets], I'm really going to be mad." When that statement was used against him in his trial, the man appealed that the remark was obtained illegally and that he was thrown off guard because the officer was laughing. The court disagreed, saying the officer had reason to laugh.

■

Secret Service agents in San Francisco had no trouble spotting the work of a currency counterfeiter because his color-blindness led him to use the wrong color ink.

All in the Family

A 36-year-old woman in Santa Ana, California, extorted more than $350,000 from her parents by claiming she had been kidnaped—150 times in two years. Each time, the daughter sent a ransom note saying she had been abducted for unpaid debts and warning her parents not to call the police.

Time and again, the dutiful couple came to her rescue, cleaning out their savings, mortgaging their property, dipping into their retirement funds and borrowing heavily from relatives. The stress finally became so much for the father that he suffered a heart attack and died while clutching one of the ransom notes. Authorities said the daughter spent the money on drugs.

■

After deciding that the world had given them a raw deal, a St. Cloud, Florida, couple signed a suicide pact. The wife went first. She shot herself in the chest with a .38-caliber pistol, then went into convulsions and died. Witnessing her pain changed the husband's mind. He strapped a seat belt around his wife's body and drove to a friend's house.

■

A onetime winner of a "Foster Parent of the Year" award was sentenced to six months in jail for sexually assaulting a 9-year-old girl who had been placed in his family's care.

After two years of marriage, a couple confessed to each other in 1979 that they wanted to be transsexuals. Although they had two children, the couple decided to seek sex-change operations. Harry, the 6-foot-8 husband, became the wife, Sheila Marie. Jean, the 5-foot-4 wife, became the husband, Thomas Eugene.

The chief of obstetrics at a Denver hospital, Dr. Paul Wexler, announced in 1979 that some generous sperm donors are fathering so many children that their offspring may someday meet and marry without knowing they're related. Wexler warned that the consequences of such generosity on society may be widespread genetic disorders.

In Crete, Illinois, an 80-year-old man confessed to beating his wife of 57 years to death with a hammer. He told police that he suffered from a heart ailment and cataracts, was afraid he would die and wanted to avoid leaving his wife a widow.

Unable to attend a birthday party that relatives had planned for her because she couldn't find a baby sitter, a teen-age mother in Chicago dropped her 39-day-old daughter down the chute of the trash incinerator-compactor at her home, then went to the party.

Police in San Jose, California, charged a 220-pound woman with crushing her 8-year-old son to death. The woman said she had been punishing the boy by sitting on his chest for three hours because a counselor advised her to "use her weight" to discipline the boy.

A couple in Leigh, England, who had been foster parents to forty-seven children were told they couldn't adopt a child of their own because their marriage was too happy. Social service officials explained to Harry and Esther Hough that a child growing up in the blissful environment of their home would receive insufficient exposure to negative experiences.

■

A Tacoma, Washington, woman received thirty days in jail for keeping her 8-year-old stepgrandson in a box for two years. She let him out only to defecate and attend church. The boy told his rescuers he was surprised to learn that all little boys aren't kept in boxes.

■

Because of an Italian law forbidding a woman who is pregnant or has a child younger than six months from being jailed, a female burglar evaded arrest and prison for seven years by having seven babies in a row. Her luck ran out in 1979 when police making a routine call found she had no medical certificate to prove she was still immune from serving a six-year sentence handed down in 1972 for a series of burglaries.

■

Police in Cushing, Oklahoma, arrested a 36-year-old Vietnam-war veteran and former mental patient who held his 76-year-old mother captive in a motel room for three months. Although the man and his mother both are white, officers said he explained he "was trying to make his mother a registered white person but that she wasn't doing the things a registered white person should do."

Smooth Reactions

A stroke victim in a Berkeley, California, hospital who was able to communicate only "yes" or "no" by blinking his eyes received a Christmas gift enabling him to "talk." The Holiday Project Mid-Peninsula Committee raised $4,000 to buy the patient a special computer with a video screen bearing selected basic sentences, such as "I'm thirsty," that can be activated with a light touch of a button on the keyboard. The patient's first message to his benefactors was, "Leave me alone."

■

An attorney arguing a malpractice suit against two doctors in Bloomsburg, Pennsylvania, had just finished telling the jury of the defendants' "lack of skill, care, diligence and good judgment," when he suddenly collapsed from an apparent heart attack. The defendants, Dr. Ala al-Mashat and Dr. Ferdinand Szabo, revived 71-year-old John Crisman with an assist from Dr. Phillip Breen, a surgeon who testified against them. When Crisman recovered after seven minutes of mouth-to-mouth resuscitation and heart stimulation, Dr. al-Mashat told him, "It's a good thing you sued good doctors."

■

Jerry Robinson, serving a life sentence in Auburn, New York, for murdering two police officers, petitioned to be released because his heart had stopped beating for two minutes during open-heart surgery—thus ending his natural life, he said, and fulfilling the sentence.

■

Anthony Tait, a four-year member of Alaska's Hells Angels, went into the Crazy Horse lounge in Anchorage and ordered a beer. The strip joint's bouncer told Tait he'd have to take off his leather jacket or leave. Tait responded to the challenge to his biker's colors by suing the bar.

■

A police psychologist in Lima, Peru, said he was so revolted by the confessions he heard from one alleged mass murderer that he took off his belt and used it to strangle the suspect in a jail cell.

■

Santa Clara County, California, Judge Joseph Biafore added six months to 300-pound David Todd Brown's two-year burglary sentence after Brown reacted to the punishment by dropping his pants and mooning the judge.

■

A neighborhood panhandler in Lansing, Michigan, asked a bank teller for 50 cents for a beer. Thinking she heard him say "give me your money," the teller emptied her cash drawer and handed over $1,300. The panhandler, who prosecutors say committed no crime, had already spent the money by the time police found him.

■

Late for his golf game, a Sebastopol, California, man rushed to join his foursome at the fourth hole. His irritated partner, who was also his best friend, greeted him by clubbing him with a 5-iron and a 7-iron, breaking his arm and bruising a kidney.

■

A Crown Point, Indiana, man became so mad when his wife got a parking ticket that he caulked shut 102 parking meters.

In France, Roland Agret, sentenced in 1973 to fifteen years in prison for murder, protested his innocence by embarking on a campaign of self-destruction. Shortly after his conviction, he swallowed forks, spoons and pens, making three stomach operations necessary. In 1974 he tried to hang himself, but a prison guard cut him down. The following year, Agret started a hunger strike that lasted 393 days. In response to the fast, his sentence was reduced, and he was freed on order of then-President Valery Giscard d'Estaing.

Agret wasn't satisfied with the pardon, however, because it didn't reverse his conviction. In 1983 he cut off one of his little fingers and carried it in a jar to the Justice Ministry. A year later he did the same with his other little finger and threatened to sew up his mouth and begin another hunger strike if he didn't get a new trial. Finally, in 1984, an appeals court ordered a new trial for the 43-year-old man.

Animal
Tales

David Lowe, a geophysicist with the New Zealand Institute of Nuclear Science has partially attributed the gradual warming of the earth's atmosphere to flatulent sheep. Noting New Zealand's 70 million sheep emit 2.5 billion gallons of methane into the atmosphere every week, he observed: "If you could hook up a sheep to the carburetor of a car, you could run it for several kilometers a day. To power the same vehicle by people, you'd need a whole football team and a couple of kegs of beer."

■

A four-ton elephant being used to help erect a circus big top in Springhill, Louisiana, was electrocuted by a power line, then fell onto its trainer, Tim Mericash, killing him instantly.

■

A pet cat that was reunited with its owner in Chelmsford, England, after a thirty-day absence leapt to greet her but clawed open a vein in the woman's leg, causing the woman to lose consciousness and die.

■

In Salem, Wisconsin, an 1,800-pound bull that had been treated as a pet killed its owner as he tried to take it to slaughter one day after the bull trampled a farmhand to death.

A female stripper was arrested in East Hartford, Connecticut, in 1984 and charged with animal cruelty and sexual assault for using a monkey in her act to help pull down the top of her dress to expose her breasts.

An eight-point buck, wounded by a deer hunter's arrow near Seymour, Wisconsin, in 1986 attacked the same hunter the following day. The animal used its sharp antlers to pin the hunter to the ground and cut the man with one of his own arrowheads.

Winds of 45 mph toppled a one-ton tree onto a tent at a county fair in Topsfield, Massachusetts. The 125 people inside escaped injury, but at the goat-judging contest, two goats fainted and had to be revived with mouth-to-mouth resuscitation.

Slick, a concrete pig installed to grunt at patrons leaving a barbecue restaurant in Boulder, Colorado, was silenced by a furious pit bull terrier. Don Ray, owner of the Oh, Carolina! Pit Barbecue, said a woman and her dog were walking past the restaurant at the same time the sensor on the exit door was activated. After six to eight grunts and snorts, the 1,500-pound pig said, "Step a little closer and let me boar you for a while."
   Ray, who was in the back of the restaurant, said the dog "went nuts and went straight for the throat. In thirty seconds, he had ripped Slick's speaker and wooden frame to shreds." By the time Ray reached the front door, the incident was over and the woman and her dog were gone. He said he found Slick's speaker on the ground, "teeth marks and all."

After raiding a liquor cabinet, a pet chimpanzee dived through the front window of its owner's house and ran drunkenly through a neighborhood in Queens, New York, breaking windows and biting a neighbor on the toe. The chimp evaded pursuing police officers for half an hour until its owner arrived and persuaded the animal to return home. Police said the chimp had downed a quart of vodka and two bottles of beer.

■

A baby pilot whale that had beached itself on Nantucket Island during a storm died despite rescue attempts of officials at the Mystic, Connecticut, Marineland Aquarium. They reported their efforts included administering heart massage and "mouth-to-blowhole resuscitation."

Weird Punishment

A high school senior in North Kingstown, Rhode Island, was disciplined for "humming and singing along" with the national anthem as it was played over the school's public address system in the morning. Administrators said school policy is to listen respectfully.

■

In Pensacola, Florida, a veterinarian was sentenced to two years' probation after pleading no contest to charges of animal cruelty. He was accused of biting a dog on the nose.

■

A former bank manager admitted administering spankings to more than fifty customers of a Pittsburgh bank in the late 1970s as punishment for falling behind on their loan payments. "I never had any trouble with them afterwards," he said.

He was later found guilty of misappropriating $88,268 in bank funds. He told the court he was forced to use the money to make unrecorded loans when six of those who were spanked threatened to report his actions to his superiors.

■

A substitute teacher in Indianapolis rewarded the well-behaved pupils in her fifth-grade class by having them line up and spit on the bad ones.

Gordon Pickrell of Kingston, Tennessee, who was pinned under his wrecked sports car for six hours with a broken arm, said the worst part of the ordeal was having to listen to the British group Wham! playing on his tape recorder the whole time. "I never want to hear it again," the teen-ager told Roane County deputies who pulled him from the overturned car. "I swear I don't."

■

A British army sergeant was accused of turning young recruits into a human xylophone by hitting them across the bare buttocks with a baseball bat as they knelt in a line. According to the prosecutor at the sergeant's court-martial, each recruit had to yell a musical note when he was hit, and the sergeant continued until he had played a tune.

■

State prison officials in Arizona announced in 1984 that they would handle inmates who continually behave "in an unacceptable manner" by serving them meat loaf for twenty-one consecutive meals. "Who says food served to incorrigible inmates has to be aesthetically attractive and tasteful?" said John Turner, a state Corrections Department spokesperson. The Arizona Civil Liberties Union challenged the get-tough policy as "cruel and unusual punishment."

■

In New Orleans, four inmates of the Orleans Parish Jail announced they were suing the sheriff for making them wear pink prison uniforms to show they had been exposed to the AIDS virus. They charged the uniforms stigmatized them and constituted cruel and unusual punishment.

■

Federal Judge John Hannum ordered a convicted drug dealer who fathered three children out of wedlock to abstain from "fornication" and "bastardy" for five years as a condition of his probation. Although Hannum didn't spell out how the sentence would be enforced, probation official Albert Christy said his office would "have to rely on the integrity of the defendant."

■

New York City's alternative sentencing program for non-violent criminals allows them to substitute such chores as sidewalk-sweeping for jail. Of the first one hundred people in the program in the early 1980s, ninety-seven chose jail.

■

Britain updated the judicial concept of an eye for an eye by deciding criminals should be forced to pay compensation to people they beat up. It gave judges a list of recommended fees for punches, including $84 for grazing a victim, $168 for causing a black eye and $2,940 for breaking a jaw that must be wired together.

■

In Carlsbad, New Mexico, a man shot the woman with whom he lived in the buttocks in 1986 because she served him green beans once too often. "Wouldn't you be mad," he asked police (who found blood and green beans strewn all over the kitchen), "if you had to eat green beans all the time?"

The Honeymoon's Over

After he apparently fell in love with one of two motel maids he held hostage during an eight-hour standoff with police in Ruston, Louisiana, the kidnaper asked for a minister to be brought to the scene to marry them. A few minutes after the fake ceremony, he surrendered.

■

James B. Burns of Houston, paralyzed from the neck down after his first wife shot him in the spine, was charged with killing his bride of two weeks with a concealed, mouth-operated pistol mounted on his wheelchair. Witnesses to the incident at the Hobo Lounge told police that Berta Mae Burns put a string in her husband's mouth, then he pulled his head back to fire the 9-mm pistol three times, shooting her in the neck.

Burns denied murdering his wife and accused her of using his handicap to commit suicide. He explained she had persuaded him to let her mount the gun on his wheelchair after a former boyfriend threatened her. The night of the shooting, Burns said, he was trying to resist her attempts to put the string in his mouth when the gun fired. He said it fired a second time when she reached for the string and a third time when he jerked backward as her body fell toward him.

Burns died two months after the incident, before the case could come to trial.

Newlyweds from Uruguay were honeymooning in New York City. After an evening on the town, the couple returned to their twentieth-floor hotel room. While engaged in horseplay with her husband, the bride stood up and bounced on the bed, which was beside a closed window. According to her husband, she lost her balance and fell, crashing through the window glass and plunging to her death.

■

Police in Miami charged a 90-year-old man with killing his 76-year-old bride of less than a week during an argument over whether the newlyweds should take a honeymoon cruise.

■

During the few minutes between their wedding and the reception, Daniel and Susan Stockwell of Basingstoke, England, decided to get a divorce. He claimed she saw him "talking innocently to an ex-girlfriend and blew her top." She told surprised guests, "It's all over."

And when Thomas Mihalko saw his bride dancing with a guest at their wedding reception, he attacked her and tore her dress. The assault charge against him was dismissed at the request of the bride, who said she would seek an annulment of her marriage.

■

A man was awaiting trial on burglary charges in northwest England when he was let out of jail under guard to get married. After the ceremony, he asked for the handcuffs to be removed while he posed for wedding pictures, then ran off as other members of the family prevented the guards from catching him.

■

Guests at a wedding reception in Lanzhou, China, heard a scream from the bedroom and rushed in to find both the bride and groom unconscious on the sofa. They were rushed to the hospital, but the bride was dead. The groom said he had been kissing his wife on the neck. According to doctors, the passion, intensity and length of the kiss caused fatal heart palpitations.

■

After the groom at a Media, Pennsylvania, wedding fought with his bride at their wedding reception, his best man's wife drove with him to his home to try to calm him down. The woman later reported that he raped her. He was convicted and sentenced to four to ten years in prison.

■

After hitchhiking from Portland, Oregon, to Reno, Nevada, to avoid a thirty-day wait to get married, a man and his bride exchanged vows at a wedding chapel on Wednesday. Hours later, he was arrested for failing to pay a $70 limousine fare.

He was sprung Friday morning by an anonymous benefactor, but after his release he couldn't find his wife. Frantic, thinking she had deserted him, he caught a taxi to look for her.

He stopped only to put a $4 deposit on a 1981 Ferrari, which cost $58,793. "We took his $4 and told him to come back when he had his financing together," said Dick Sims, co-owner of Modern Classic Motors.

After resuming his search, but before finding his wife or getting his financing together, he was back in jail—unable to pay a $21 taxi fare.

■

In Syracuse, New York, a 34-year-old man who beat his first wife to death in 1977 admitted in 1984 to stabbing his second wife of less than a year in the chest while she was sleeping. When she awoke and started fighting back, he hit her on the head with a board, then had sex with her before calling an ambulance an hour later. According to the police, when they arrived he said, "I stabbed my wife. I am on parole for killing my first wife, and I know I am going to get in trouble for this."

Medical Milestones

John Tingstedt was released from the Gallipolis, Ohio, Developmental Center in 1986 after being confined there for thirty-nine years for treatment of epilepsy—even though the 77-year-old man had no symptoms of the disorder.

■

A Bangladesh surgeon told a 1988 conference of the Asian Association of Pediatric Surgeons how ordinary paper clips, when bent into proper shapes, can substitute for expensive surgical equipment. "In a poor and developing country," he said, "the paper clip has been our answer."

■

The medical director of a hospital in Puerto Rico was paid more than $22,000 by two drug companies to test two diarrhea medicines to determine their safety and effectiveness, then submitted phony data to the drug companies and the federal Food and Drug Administration. Although he claimed to have tried one of the drugs on more than sixty children at the hospital, FDA investigator Doralie L. Segal said she made three trips to Puerto Rico but could not find one child who actually took the drug. One 37-month-old boy he claimed to have treated for diarrhea turned out to be a 23-month-old boy who had never had the malady and who had gone to the hospital to have a flower removed from his nose.

■

A British medical journal contained a story about a spinal defect that causes victims to stand like apes. The story was illustrated with side-by-side photos of an ape and a slouching human. As is common practice, the human's identity was protected by a black square superimposed over his face. There was also one over the ape's face.

■

The California Board of Medical Examiners censured a Glendale surgeon for removing the left breast of a 9-year-old patient after failing to recognize the girl was going through puberty. The doctor, who operated on the girl in 1979, told the board he thought the girl might have had an abscess or a tumor and that he meant to remove only a piece of tissue for examination. He said he realized too late that his diagnosis was wrong and the surgery unnecessary.

■

Donald Wright, 54, was installing a sliding door in his apartment building in downtown Toronto when he fell off a stepladder and knocked himself out. He regained consciousness to find that he'd fallen on a power drill whose bit bored three inches into his right temple. "I tried to pull it out but it wouldn't come out," Wright said. "So I knew the only way to get it out was by restarting it."

He got up and carried the five-pound drill into the bathroom. "I looked into the mirror and restarted the drill and pulled it out of my head," he said. Bleeding profusely, Wright was taken to the hospital, where he underwent surgery to remove a bone fragment from his brain. "I guess it just wasn't my turn to die," he said afterwards.

■

Baseball player Jamie Allen, whose professional career was riddled with injuries, found himself out of action again after an incident at the Seattle Mariners' spring training camp in 1983. Allen said he suffered a pulled groin muscle when he crossed his legs while watching television.

■

Boston Celtics broadcaster Johnny Most went to the doctor for an examination to see why he was having trouble hearing. The doctor checked his ear and found a radio ear plug, which had been in Most's ear for eighteen months.

■

According to a Harvard University research team, 280,000 Americans died from cancer in 1962. Twenty years later, cancer claimed 435,000 lives. The researchers concluded that the nation's massively expensive war on cancer has to be considered "a qualified failure."

■

Doctors at a University of Pittsburgh—affiliated hospital finally were able to resolve a long-standing medical dispute about the best way to remove live cockroaches that crawl into the ears of sleeping people. One faction of the medical profession had held that mineral oil was the most effective. Another group had argued for a 2 percent solution of lidocaine, a local anesthetic.

The opportunity to compare the effectiveness of both methods arose when a patient arrived at the hospital's emergency room with a roach in each ear. Doctors placed a few drops of mineral oil in one ear, then had to struggle to remove the insect successfully. They sprayed lidocaine in the other ear, and the roach quickly exited the ear canal.

■

Dr. J. Brendan Wynne, a Philadelphia orthopedic surgeon, wrote the *Journal of the American Medical Association* to alert doctors and the public to possible dangers of vacuum toilets, which are common aboard ships and airplanes. He related that in 1986 he was vacationing aboard the cruise ship *Pegasus* when he responded to an emergency call. He found a 70-year-old woman lying on a bunk with "several feet of small intestine" trailing behind her. Wynne said that the slightly obese woman, alert but obviously in pain, told him she had flushed the toilet while seated and the suction had "pulled everything out."

■

In 1985, Scottish psychologist Reginald Passmore identified an eating disorder stemming from fear of modern foods. He called the syndrome "trophophobia." He said it is "engendered by the constant media barrage that makes people believe modern foods are poisonous, allergy producing, inadequate and so forth."

■

Dale Eller, 22, of Columbus, Ohio, walked into police headquarters and requested an X-ray in order to locate his brain. He showed the police a hole in his skull through which he had inserted three inches of wire trying to find his brain but had failed. He told them he had made the hole with a power drill.

Police took Eller to the hospital, where doctors removed a coat hanger wire from his head. A hospital official said Eller was in good condition, although doctors said he might have personality changes.

Penis Envy

In Plymouth, England, Dr. Peter Gibbs of the Marine Biological Association reported that female dog whelks were growing penises and developing sperm ducts. He attributed the phenomenon to water pollution caused by tributyltin, an anti-foulant ingredient of paint used on boat hulls. Gibbs said he found that when the whelks' shells were painted with the chemical, "penises sprouted and grew to alarming lengths."

■

Dr. Mario Degni, a specialist in sexual impotence in Sao Paolo, Brazil, announced development of a new surgical technique for lengthening the penis that could offer relief to the millions of men traumatized by the diminutive size of their organs. He said he conducted two successful operations, adding an average of one-half inch, and that the patients resumed sexual activity within a month of the surgery. Even before the announcement, Degni had been named "Surgeon of the Century" by the U.S. International College of Surgeons.

■

Two dozen Nigerian fishermen tried to lynch witch doctor Ibrahim Hassane, claiming he used magic to reduce the size of their penises by two-thirds. After the police prevented the lynching, the fishermen showed officers their diminished genitals. The police say Hassane acknowledged responsibility but wouldn't explain how he performed his magic.

■

The National Organization of Circumcision Information Resource Centers designated 1987 the "Year of the Intact Child." The California-based group also named the Prince and Princess of Wales "parents of the year" for their decision to leave Princes William and Henry "intact and non-circumcised— even though their father, Prince Charles, was circumcised at birth."

■

Surgeons at Yale–New Haven Hospital in Connecticut successfully re-attached the penis of a 32-year-old man who accidentally amputated the organ with a circular saw while cutting wood in his basement. Dr. Charles Cuono, who headed the team that performed the eight-hour operation, said the man had "at least a fifty-fifty chance his sexual functions will be restored."

■

Four months before he was to be married in 1974, a man was admitted to North Hills Passavant Hospital in Pennsylvania for surgery to correct a recessed testicle. During the relatively routine operation a doctor accidentally amputated the future groom's penis. The man was awarded $825,000 in an out-of-court settlement.

■

A man serving time for a rape he says he didn't commit won $195,000 from a Helena, Arkansas, jury for emotional distress over the actions of a local sheriff. After a vigilante squad had castrated the accused rapist before his arrest in 1987, the sheriff, who was not one of the vigilantes, seized the testicles and allegedly displayed them in a jar in his office for visitors to see. The convicted man said the action violated his privacy.

■

In Bangkok, Thailand, 1,214 men received free vasectomies to celebrate King Bhumibol Adulyadej's sixtieth birthday in 1987. Promoters of the voluntary vasectomies claimed a world record. The previous record, also claimed by Thailand, was 1,202, set in 1983.

■

A man charged with raping a 14-year-old Jacksonville, Florida, girl in 1984 contended at his trial that he couldn't have committed the crime because his penis was 9 inches long. The examining physician testified that a violently thrusting 9-inch penis would likely cause vaginal lacerations and that he had found no such lacerations when he examined the victim.

Judge James L. Harrison balked at allowing introduction of photographs of the defendant's penis, although the defense argued that this evidence was central to its case. Harrison did let the photographer testify that the defendant's penis was 9 inches long, but he refused to admit testimony that its circumference measured 5½ inches. The judge also refused to admit a wooden model of the penis and rejected a defense request that the defendant be permitted to show the jury his organ.

■

Sweden's Health Ministry Ethics Committee chastised a hospital nurse and a surgeon who mistakenly removed a patient's testicle. The error occurred when two men were scheduled for urological operations in adjacent rooms, one for prostrate cancer and the other for minor exploratory surgery. To avoid any mix-up, the nurse gave each patient a number—only she gave both the same number. When the surgeon got to the number, he assumed the patient was the one with cancer and quickly cut off one testicle. He was about to remove the other testicle when someone noticed the patient was the one scheduled for exploratory surgery.

Handicapable

Virginia state trooper R.L. Farney pulled over a weaving car early one morning and found that its driver wasn't just drunk but also blind. Farney reported that the man explained he was driving because his woman companion "was drunker than he was." The driver added that she had been directing him. "He thought he was driving OK," said Farney, who disagreed and ticketed both of them.

■

An unidentified man in a wheelchair rolled into a gas station in Freeport, New York, hastily assembled a rifle in front of two teen-agers running the station, and demanded cash. After the boys handed over $200, the man forced one of them to push him two blocks to safety.

■

In 1973, West Nyack, New York, responded to a Supreme Court decision letting local communities set their own standards of obscenity by establishing a committee to screen movies, cabaret acts, and printed material. The nine-member panel selected as its head Marty Snyder, a 60-year-old blind man. "Pornography isn't a case of seeing," Snyder said. "It's a case of feeling." He explained he would be able to scrutinize movies by listening to the dialogue and having other members sit next to him to "fill me in when the screen goes silent."

■

A South Carolina appeals court ruled that a one-legged bingo player who couldn't hobble fast enough to claim her prize was not entitled to it. Delores Taylor testified that she began hollering "bingo" as soon as her winning number was called, but the caller didn't hear her. She hobbled up to an usher to try and stop another number from being called. She failed, and three other winners claimed the prize on the next number.

■

Government lawyers charged that for six years a Columbus, Ohio, auto parts company used blind workers to remove "Made in Japan" stickers from parts and re-pack them in cases marked "Made in U.S.A."

■

A blind man held up a London bank but was caught while trying to make his getaway when he couldn't distinguish the bank's glass windows from its glass door.

■

In Narooma, Australia, 16-year-old Greg Hammond, who was born with only one hand, placed second in a men's 100-meter race. Officials disqualified him, however, after an appeal noted that he failed to touch the end of the pool with both hands as specified by international rules.

■

In New Bedford, Massachusetts, a 77-year-old woman confined to a wheelchair was charged with murdering her 80-year-old husband. Before he died, he told police his wife constantly hit him with a walking cane, a glass vase and other objects over a three-day period. He added she didn't allow him to sleep during that time; when he tried, she grabbed his genitals and pulled, squeezed and twisted them until he no longer could stand the pain. Investigators said his left foot was almost double its normal size and his genital area was "swollen to the size of a small balloon."

■

Police in Franklin Township, New Jersey, charged a 25-year-old paraplegic with robbing an elderly couple. He broke into their house, pulled himself through it with his hands and stole $140 after telling the couple he had a gun.

■

Little League Inc. of Williamsport, Pennsylvania, refused to sanction a league for disabled youngsters in Brockton, Massachusetts. The organization also threatened to revoke the charter of all that city's Little Leagues unless they officially severed ties with the teams that carried players with Down's syndrome and multiple sclerosis.

■

A winner of Michigan's Homemaker of the Year, who also suffered from multiple sclerosis and was confined to a wheelchair, was charged with murdering her husband with a 22-caliber rifle as he lay in bed.

■

When an inveterate bank robber had to have his right leg amputated at the hip while serving a prison term, his hold-up days seemed over. But as soon as he was released on parole, he hobbled into the Farmers and Merchants Bank of Bumpus Mills, Tennessee, and emptied the cash drawers at gunpoint.

■

A muffler shop manager in West Springfield, Massachusetts, wouldn't accept Donald Vadnais's credit card to pay for repairs because it was his mother's, so Vadnais left his artificial arm as collateral. "I didn't want to keep the guy's arm," the shop manager said, "but he didn't seem to mind."

Litigious Society

A couple from Berlin Heights, Ohio, filed a $125,000 lawsuit against a pizza company, claiming a "spoiled, rotten, rancid and moldy" pizza caused the death of their dog Fluffy. Their lawyer said the couple "became violently ill after eating a small quantity of the pizza. Then they became severely distressed in their search for medical assistance and ran over Fluffy in the driveway."

■

A 305-pound Virginia man who underwent a stomach-stapling operation in 1984 to try to lose weight filed a $250,000 lawsuit against the hospital where the surgery was performed. He contended it was negligent for allowing him near a refrigerator, which he raided two days after the surgery, eating so much that he popped his staples and had to undergo emergency surgery.

■

An Arizona jury awarded a Tucson woman $356,250 in damages for injuries she suffered when she fell out of the jury box while serving as a juror.

■

A federal appeals court in 1979 ruled against four Maryland men who contended that they should be exempt from paying federal income tax because they were descended from slaves.

The four had argued that slaves in this country were never legally raised from the status of property and that following emancipation slaves were never compensated for their bondage. The three-judge panel said the Thirteenth and Fourteenth Amendments in effect made former slaves U.S. citizens and thus liable for taxes.

A 28-year-old man who drove his car down the wrong side of a highway in Pontiac, Michigan, and struck another car head-on, killing Sigmund and Irene Fitz, filed suit seeking damages from their estate. He told a jury his life had fallen apart since the 1976 accident and that he often feels he would be better off dead. His attorney added that his client was entitled to damages because the driver of the Fitz car was partially at fault for not swerving out of his way before the collision.

A court in Ontario, Canada, awarded a 29-year-old man $13,000 in a lawsuit against the estate of his mother, who died in 1986. He contended that in 1984 after he asked her to dance, she started to rise but then negligently fell on him, breaking his ankle.

A Concord, California, woman sued the International House of Pancakes restaurant near her home for not participating in IHOP's national "Sweet 16" breakfast special. She alleged a "burning in the stomach from hunger" and severe emotional distress, humiliation and disappointment—to the tune of $2 billion.

A California state trooper was dismissed after seven women co-workers complained that he "made them feel uncomfortable by his prolonged staring at them and their body parts." The former state trooper sued, arguing that he made no sexual comments and hadn't touched the women. The California Court of Appeals ruled that his firing was justified, however, calling his habit of staring at women "annoying and frightening."

■

When Roberta Sahr began choking in a New York City restaurant, a quick-acting cashier used the Heimlich maneuver to dislodge the food in her throat. Later, Sahr complained of stomach pains and was hospitalized She died three weeks later of a ruptured stomach.

Her daughter filed suit against the restaurant's owner, contending that Sahr hadn't been choking at all, merely trying to catch her breath. "The cashier meant well," the daughter said, "but he killed my mother."

■

The U.S. District Court in Washington, D.C., banished a man who filed 110 lawsuits over a two-year period from filing any further suits. He once sued a drugstore in New York City for $500 billion because a clerk threatened to throw him out of the store. He also sought "$100 zillion" in damages from a Maryland roller rink where he was refused admission.

■

When a Rockville, Maryland, woman sued her employer for $500,000 for injuries from falling off a chair at work, the company produced a witness who testified the woman had been practicing falling off chairs at work "for years."

■

A supermarket clerk in Gresham, Oregon, sued a co-worker for $100,000 for mental stress and humiliation. He charged the colleague with "repeatedly and intentionally" passing gas at him while both were clerks in a local supermarket.

■

The Episcopal bishop of Central Florida sued the U.S. government for $200,000. He claimed that a knee injury he suffered on the Naval Training Center's tennis courts prevented him from genuflecting. The government countersued, claiming that the bishop trespassed by playing his matches early in the morning to avoid detection.

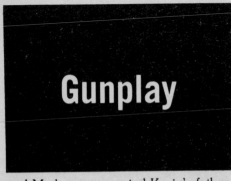

Gunplay

Two teen-agers, Kevin and Mark, accompanied Kevin's father from Chicago to Winston-Salem, North Carolina, to watch Kevin's kid brother play football. While waiting in their motel, the two boys drank beer and watched television for several hours, then Kevin pulled a pistol from a suitcase. Thinking it was empty, he joked, "Watch, I'm going to kill myself," but when he pulled the trigger, the gun fired, shooting him in the forehead.

"What luck," said Kevin's brother when he learned his brother had been hospitalized in critical condition. "First we lose the football game, and then this happens."

■

Elaine Cunningham of San Diego, California, was shot in both arms when a friend's husband dropped his pants and bent over to pose for a photograph at a picnic, causing a pistol to fall from his belt and accidentally go off.

■

A man in Johannesburg, South Africa, shot his 49-year-old friend in the face, seriously wounding him, while the two practiced shooting beer cans off each other's head.

■

A 35-year-old New Jersey man got mad at his home computer, so he pulled out a .44-Magnum automatic and pumped eight shots into it, blowing out the monitor screen and blasting the computer's inner workings. He used hollow-point, or dum-dum, bullets. Police Lt. Donald VanTassel, calling the handgun "quite a lot of firepower for the job," said the man was surprised when the police arrested him because he "didn't understand why he couldn't shoot his own computer in his own house."

■

M.C. Russell, who was shot more than twenty years earlier during a fight with his wife, died in 1988 from the bullet that lodged in his spine and left him nearly bedridden. Doctors couldn't re-move the bullet for fear of causing more spinal damage. The Dallas County, Texas, medical examiner ruled the death a homicide, but investigators closed the case almost immediately because Russell's wife Lois, whom he had divorced, died in 1984.

■

Two men in Manila were shot dead for arguing that the chicken came before the egg. Philippine newspapers reported four pro-ponents for the egg took out their pistols and shot their oppo-nents after one of the chicken-firsters, thinking his view had won, made an obscene gesture.

■

A Bellevue, Washington, man, frustrated after his car got stuck, took a tire iron out of his trunk and smashed every window in the car. Still not satisfied, he pulled out a .9-mm pistol and shot all four tires full of holes. The man then reloaded the gun and fired several more shots, but the weapon jammed. He threw it down in the snow and returned to the tire iron. He was battering the hood when the police arrived. They said the man appeared sober and rational, just extremely perturbed.

■

In Houston, Texas, two friends shot and killed each other in a bar after arguing over how easy it was to get away with mur-der in the city. Witnesses told the police that James Cole claimed it was easy to escape arrest for murder, whereas Harold Kirkley argued a victim could retaliate by shooting back. Cole picked up a pistol, saying he wasn't sure it worked, and fired, hitting Kirkley, who pulled out a pistol and shot Cole.

■

Seven bridegrooms in northern Pakistan were arrested for "lethal celebrations during marriage ceremonies" in connection with the 1986 crash of a Pakistan International Airlines plane in which thirteen people died and more than twenty were injured. Authorities said that villagers firing rifles into the air—a common feature of weddings in the region—may have caused the accident by hitting the aircraft or distracting the pilot.

■

A 15-year-old boy in Riga, New York, who said he was upset that Syracuse University's basketball team lost to Pittsburgh, spent five hours shooting up his house with assorted rifles and handguns. Monroe County sheriff's deputies who talked the boy into surrendering estimated he fired at least 300 rounds of ammunition.

The house was "a shambles," sheriff's spokesman Thomas Ryan said. "He shot out the television, the stove, the walls, the ceilings, windows, sliding glass doors, a water pipe which ruptured and squirted water everywhere, and even the electrical box in the basement."

■

A 24-year-old woman in Dallas, Texas, got angry when two men tried to repossess her washing machine and started shooting at them after they carried the washer out of her house. They abandoned the machine in the yard and ran off. Then she turned around and began shooting the washer. One bullet missed the machine or ricocheted and killed her 7-year-old nephew.

■

Police in Charleston, South Carolina, arrested a man who handed a note demanding money to the automatic teller machine at a bank. A police officer who witnessed the incident said that when the machine didn't respond to the demand, the man pumped two shots into it and drove off.

Ray County, Missouri, conservation agent George Hiser told his wife to take her best shot when a turkey came out of the woods while they were hunting. Marcia Hiser not only dropped the bird at 40 yards, but she also hit a second turkey 15 yards behind it with the same blast. Since Missouri law prohibits killing more than one turkey a week during the spring season, George had no choice but to issue Marcia a ticket.

Oops

Swedish business consultant Ulf af Trolle labored thirteen years on a book about Swedish economic solutions. He took the 250-page manuscript to be copied, only to have it reduced to 50,000 strips of paper in seconds when a worker confused a copier with a shredder.

■

The Washington Post printed a story about policy changes being proposed for the U.S. Labor Department. Beneath a man's photo accompanying the article was the caption: "Labor official who briefed reporters under a condition his name not be used."

■

The Georgia State Game Commission spent a considerable amount of time debating the regulation of alligator rides before someone noticed the typographical error and realized the commission was supposed to be debating whether to regulate alligator hides.

■

In Tokyo, explosive chemicals in a model volcano being prepared for a school exhibit blew up, injuring seventeen high school students.

A_n Oklahoma City jury needed just twenty minutes to decide that a few words from the unwise were sufficient to convict the defendant of armed robbery, despite his claim of an alibi. His court-appointed attorney was questioning the victim, who identified the defendant as the robber. The defendant jumped to his feet and accused the witness of lying. "I should have blown your . . . head off," he said, quickly adding, "If I'd been the one that was there."

■

A Northwest Airlines flight from Seattle to Detroit made an emergency landing in Salt Lake City after the crew smelled gasoline. Investigators discovered the fumes came from a West German tourist who brought an empty gas can aboard after his car had run out of gas on the way to the Seattle airport.

■

I_n a Wilmington, Delaware, trial, the defendant was acting as his own lawyer after denying that he had robbed a woman clerk at a Texaco station. He was cross-examining a detective who referred to the clerk as a witness. "What are you talking about some witness, man?" he challenged. "There was only me and her in the store."

■

E_xperienced skydiver Ivan Lester McGuire loaded up with portable video equipment to record a dive near Louisburg, North Carolina, but apparently forgot to pack his parachute. After McGuire plunged to his death, a tape of the dive was recovered, showing him flailing his arms on discovering his oversight.

■

T_he West Virginia highway department built a two-lane bridge for a three-lane section of the state turnpike. Department spokesman John Gallagher blamed designers for the error, which officials didn't notice until the bridge was actually built. "It sounds a lot worse than it is," Gallagher added.

■

Members attending a Maryland Library Association convention were surprised to find that the biggest exhibit was one displaying Sanyo massage devices. Librarians entering MLA's exhibition hall were invited to step into a booth, take off their shoes, and have their feet massaged. The mystery ended when someone noticed the sign, "Sanyo improves your circulation." It turned out that Sanyo's public relations department had noticed the word "circulation" in an index to conventions and assumed the 'M' in "MLA" stood for "Medical."

■

Fire fighters in Alameda, California, rescued a 55-year-old woman who had spent five days stuck between her bed and dresser. They said she slipped off the bed and couldn't get up.

■

Richard Dickerson of Miami Beach, Florida, set off nine bug bombs to rid his apartment of cockroaches while he was on vacation. As he was leaving, the oven pilot light ignited the insecticide gas, shattering the door and windows and hurling one wall into the next apartment. Not wanting to miss his vacation, Dickerson left his neighbor $750 to repair the wall that used to separate their apartments and then took off.

■

Dee and Daniel Sweeney hired a cameraman to videotape their wedding in Bradenton, Florida. When the Sweeneys viewed the finished tape, they discovered that following the wedding sequence were 70 minutes of the cameraman nude playing with himself. He had mistakenly taped the wedding over a personal tape.

■

Engineer Donald Silk hailed Gardner, Massachusetts, police officer Robert Babineau to say his train had slipped away without him when he left it to buy a candy bar. The two men raced through three towns at breakneck speed trying to catch the train at crossings. Meanwhile, the runaway train careened out of control for thirty miles until it was deliberately crashed by dispatchers into a row of empty boxcars.

■

After last-minute campaigning to retain his seat on the Massachusetts Governor's council, Herbert Connolly raced to the polling place but arrived fifteen minutes too late to cast his ballot in the 1988 Democratic primary. The final tally was 14,715 for Connolly and 14,716 for his opponent.

■

Lawyer Reginald Tucker, 29, was at a party on the thirty-ninth floor of Chicago's Prudential Building when he took off his glasses and started racing through the corridors with a co-worker. At the end of one corridor was a window, which Tucker apparently didn't see. He kept running, crashed through the window, and plunged to his death.

Insolent Chariots

General Motors notified owners of 1988 Buick LeSabres that the owner's manual should be replaced because of a printing error. The notice came with a corrected manual and an advisory: "Please place the [new] Owner's Manual in your vehicle's 'glove box' and discard the old manual or take [the new manual] to your dealer for installation, at no charge to you. Estimated time for this correction is five (5) minutes." Syndicated columnist Mike Royko called a Chicago Buick dealer who told him that two owners had brought their manuals in for installation.

■

Korey Cragg fled his home in Hesperia, California, while sheriff's deputies tried to question him about why he had buried more than a dozen cars and trucks on his desert property.

■

After the police pulled him over, a motorist in Edmonton, Alberta, jumped out of his car, ripped out a radar detector, threw it on the ground, stomped on it and said, "I paid $500 for this damn thing, and it doesn't work." The police then explained they had stopped him for having only one license plate.

■

Betty Tudor, 60, of Exeter, England, took 273 driving lessons over nineteen years but still couldn't pass the exam to get her driver's license. "I'm a disaster when I'm driving," she admitted.

Following one test, her examiner was admitted to a mental hospital, though Tudor didn't think that she was totally to blame. Another time, she upset her instructor when she went the wrong way around a traffic circle. "I told him if it hadn't been for the cars coming in the opposite direction sounding their horns, he wouldn't have noticed anything wrong," she said. After seven tries, she announced in 1981 that she was selling her car and getting a moped, which doesn't require a license.

■

A woman in Bethesda, Maryland, who pulled into a circular driveway in front of a school, accidentally locked her keys in the car with the motor running. As she got out of the car, she slammed the door, jarring the transmission from park to reverse. The car backed around the driveway for 2½ hours before a towtruck operator stopped it by picking it up with his truck's sling.

In a similar case in 1984, 74-year-old Curtis B. Hodson of Chickasha, Oklahoma, got out of his car to toss some trash in a dumpster. He apparently left the car in reverse with the engine running and a door open. The car backed past him, and the open door knocked him to the ground. The car continued backward in a circle, running over Hodson three times before a store manager stopped it.

■

A woman in Atwood, Illinois, was taking her driving test when she put her car in reverse and backed into a tree at the examining facility. According to the police, the 77-year-old woman then put the car in forward, accelerated, jumped the curb and flew through the plate glass window of the building, killing one person and injuring four others, including the examiner in the car. She was unhurt but failed the test.

A Clovis, New Mexico, man told the authorities he was parking his car in his garage when his foot slipped off the brake and hit the accelerator. The car leapt through the garage door, hit a freezer kept inside the garage and pushed it through the wall. The freezer fell on his wife who was sitting on the other side of the wall listening to records. She died instantly.

A road grader ran out of control in Virginia Beach, Virginia, spilled its operator, ran over him, sped full throttle into an automobile showroom and destroyed three cars, then crashed into six boats at an adjacent dealership before stalling.

In Canada, a woman was charged with hiring a hit man to kill a 19-year-old neighbor because she was tired of his mufflerless Pontiac roaring through her neighborhood. The police also suspected her of poisoning her husband for threatening to turn her in for hiring the hit man.

California Highway Patrol officer Donna Urqidi observed a 1978 Volkswagen driving very slowly about 30 miles west of Los Angeles and pulled it over to investigate. When she approached the car, however, it pulled away. Urqidi gave chase, joined by another CHP patrol car and a Los Angeles police helicopter. The chase, which never exceeded the speed limit, ended four hours and 200 miles later in San Diego County when the VW ran out of gas.

Celebrity Corner

Lou Proctor was listed in the first six editions of the *Baseball Encyclopedia* as a member of the 1912 St. Louis Browns. Researchers cut short Proctor's one-game career when they discovered he was actually a press-box telegraph operator who decided one day to enter his name in the box score.

■

On a flight to Europe to kick off a concert tour, Michael Jackson reportedly wore a veil the whole time except to eat, and he did that in the first-class lavatory because he didn't want anyone to see him eating.

■

The Rev. Al Sharpton sought to confront New York Gov. Mario Cuomo at Cuomo's hotel in Atlanta during the 1988 Democratic National Convention to criticize the governor's handling of the Tawana Brawley case. Sharpton arrived an hour and a half late for his appointment, however. On learning that Cuomo had long since departed, Sharpton griped, "He should have waited around. He knew we were on our way."

■

A man charged with kidnaping and sexual battery in Tampa, Florida, agreed to a plea bargain, but the judge halted the defendant's courtroom confession when the man began to implicate Larry Hagman, Victoria Principal and Sylvester Stallone in his plan to kidnap a 7-year-old girl.

■

In Augusta, Georgia, the lawyer for Adrienne Brown, wife of soul singer James Brown, asked a judge to dismiss traffic charges against his client because she claimed "diplomatic immunity" —stemming from a 1968 tribute by a congressman who hailed the singer as "our No. 1 ambassador."

■

Seventieth-birthday congratulations received by Romanian dictator Nicolae Ceausescu from Britain's Queen Elizabeth, Sweden's King Carl Gustav and Spain's King Juan Carlos were fabricated by Ceausescu's staff because none of the monarchs had responded to requests for congratulations.

■

A newspaper carrier delivering the *Los Angeles Times* in 1984 heaved a copy toward the front lawn of actress Barbara Bain. The paper landed on her pet dog of fourteen years and killed it. A subsequent report by the newspaper industry noted that the *Times* is the fattest U.S. newspaper, averaging 2.3 pounds a day.

■

Jeb Stuart Magruder went from seven months in jail for his Watergate misdeeds to being appointed head of the Columbus, Ohio, Commission on Values and Ethics.

■

Autograph expert Herman Darvick cautioned Ronald Reagan fans that autographs from his Hollywood days probably aren't genuine. Darvick said Reagan paid his mother Nelle $75 a week to do the signing for him. In fact, he added, "she even signed Jane Wyman's name."

■

In one of his pleas for money, evangelist Oral Roberts urged his followers to scribble the name of Jesus on the soles of their shoes. "As you put your foot down, know by your faith you're bruising the devil's head," his letter said. "The devil should always see the sole of your shoe coming down on him." The letter featured a white space for contributors to outline their shoes. Within a week of Robert's letter being mailed, fellow evangelist Billy Graham was admitted to a Rochester, N.Y, hospital with a foot infection.

■

Movie actress Mamie Van Doren revealed in her autobiography, *Playing the Field*, that Henry Kissinger's socks were "smelly."

■

Just before sending off the final tape of the 1987 television movie *The Rise and Fall of the Third Reich*, the National Captioning Institute discovered that one of its editors, apparently unfamiliar with Nazi Germany, had typed for the crowd chant after every salute "Hi, Hitler!" instead of "Heil, Hitler!"

■

In a Manila suburb, a man stabbed and killed his brother and wounded their friend when they failed to agree with him that former Philippines first lady Imelda R. Marcos is prettier than Britain's Princess Diana.

Occupational Hazards

The resident safety expert for the Kansas Fish and Game Commission, who was wearing an orange cap with "Kansas Safe Hunter" printed on the front and fluorescent orange clothing, was shot accidentally in the arm and shoulder while bird hunting—by a co-worker.

■

A fist fight broke out between two surgeons during an operation at Arrowe Park Hospital in Birkenhead, England, when they clashed over working hours. One of the doctors had to be treated for minor injuries while a junior physician stepped in and finished the operation.

■

A company trying to continue its five-year perfect safety record showed its workers a film aimed at encouraging the use of safety goggles on the job. According to *Industrial Machinery News*, the film's depiction of gory industrial accidents was so graphic that twenty-five workers suffered minor injuries in their rush to leave the screening room. Thirteen others fainted, and one man required seven stitches after he cut his head falling off a chair while watching the film.

■

In Laguna Hills, California, Brinks guard Hrand Arakilian, 34, was crushed to death while riding in the back of an armored car when $13,000 in quarters, weighing 832 pounds, fell on him.

■

A high school teacher in Fairfax, Virginia, was transferred to an administrative job when it was found that the videotape on China he had left for a substitute teacher to show his students was recorded over a film of gay male sex, several scenes of which remained on the tape.

■

A Toronto restaurant owner was stabbed to death after a singer performing at the restaurant didn't know the words to a song a customer requested. The singer, a 70-year-old entertainer from Hong Kong, was taking requests at Philip's Chopsticks Restaurant, owned by Philip Yin San Wu. When a patron and his three friends sent up $20 and a request, the singer laughingly admitted he didn't know the song and said he was going to sing another number for someone who had sent up $40.

The patron claimed he had lost face and got into a scuffle with Wu. After the fight apparently ended, the patron ran into the kitchen, grabbed a butcher's knife and a meat cleaver, rushed at Wu and stabbed him repeatedly. He fled from the restaurant, but surrendered five months later. Although he said at his trial that he grabbed the weapons only to scare Wu, he was sentenced to life imprisonment.

■

Cellist Augustinas Vassiliauskas of the Soviet Vilnius string quartet was climbing the podium at the 1980 Kuhmo Music Festival for a third round of applause when he tripped and fell on his prized Ruggieri cello, breaking the 300-year-old instrument beyond repair.

■

Phil Klusman, a sportswriter for the *Bakersfield Californian*, died while covering a 1986 track and field championship in Los

Angeles after being struck in the head by a 16-pound hammer thrown by one of the athletes. Klusman had tried to protect himself from the errant throw by putting a clipboard above his head.

■

Mark Wagstaff, 30, co-owner of a company that makes security equipment, was demonstrating a bulletproof vest and asked his friend to try to stab him in the chest. The man's first attempt failed, but the second pierced Wagstaff's vest, killing him.

■

John Ramsey was loading coleslaw ingredients into a blender at Manor Hill Food Corp. in Baltimore when he slipped into the machine and was killed. And in Pico Rivera, California, food factory worker Arturo Crisostomo was accidentally crushed to death in a 5-foot deep, 10-foot long mixing bowl that he was cleaning when another employee turned on the beater.

■

Watt Espy, 54, a self-appointed historian of capital punishment, spent seventeen years compiling information about 15,459 executions in the United States since 1608 before his work finally got to him. The Headland, Alabama, resident announced that he was willing to sell his collection of index cards, ledgers and pictures of executed criminals. "Believe me, the stress is awful," said the chain smoker, who suffers from ulcers. "I'm depressed half the time."

Odd Ends

In Toronto, Franco Brun choked to death on a pocket Bible. The medical examiner speculated that the 22-year-old man had tried to swallow the 874-page Bible to purge himself of the Devil.

■

Ray Priestley of Melbourne, Australia, was trying to make the snooker shot of a lifetime—hanging upside down from a rafter over the pool table—when he slipped and hit the concrete floor. He later died from brain damage.

■

In Kuala Lampur, Malaysia, Gan Keng Woong stumbled and fell unconscious while playing badminton. The fall jarred his dentures loose, and they lodged in his windpipe, suffocating him.

■

In 1982, two relatives of an elderly Louisiana man hooked up to a kidney dialysis machine got into an argument. To stop the dispute, the man waved a gun at the pair, but it accidentally fired. The bullet pierced a tube from the dialysis machine, and the man bled to death.

■

A man who ate breakfast at the Bee Hive Restaurant in downtown Baltimore in 1979 walked out without paying the $3.43

check. Police said that when the man got outside, he took off running, then darted between two parked cars into the street, where a tractor-trailer crushed him to death.

■

In Virginia, a nearly blind 70-year-old man died during a shootout with the police that was set up by a citizens' band radio operator. In a radio argument that was recorded by other CB radio operators, the 70-year-old exchanged obscene insults and death threats with another man, who dared him to step onto his porch, gun in hand. He told the 70-year-old he was coming in a blue-and-white car to blow him up with a hand grenade.

Instead of going to the 70-year-old's house, the other CB operator called the police and told them there was a man on the porch at the 70-year-old's address waving a pistol. When the police arrived in blue-and-white cruisers, the 70-year-old fired and was killed by the officers' return fire. A Roanoke jury convicted the CB operator of involuntary manslaughter.

■

At least twenty-two members of a wedding party in Islamabad, Pakistan in 1984, drowned when fifty-two wedding guests, trying to save fares, crammed into a small fishing boat meant to carry only five, and the boat capsized.

■

In Chicago, two jilted men fell to their deaths from apartment buildings within a half-hour of each other while climbing in to see their girlfriends. Dale Moll, 33, fell sixteen stories while trying to use television cables on the roof to rappel down to the window of his girlfriend's fifteenth-floor apartment. Robert Harris, 25, fell from an eighth-story ledge while trying to get into his apartment after his girlfriend locked him out following an argument.

Three months before the twin plummet, a 25-year-old Chicago man who apparently thought his girlfriend was refusing to answer her door tried to enter from a window ledge and fell seven stories to his death. The woman wasn't home.

■

An 81-year-old woman in Arkwright, South Carolina, died of smoke inhalation after apparently mistaking an end table in her mobile home for a fireplace and setting a fire under it.

■

Utah farmer Sheldon Roberts, his teen-age son Steven and Beaver County Sheriff Dale Nelson all died after they were overcome by methane fumes from a liquid manure pit. Investigators said the first victim was trapped after entering the 10-foot-deep shaft to retrieve a fallen lid. After notifying the sheriff's office, the second victim went into the pit to attempt a rescue, but was also asphyxiated by the gas. When Nelson arrived, he tried to rescue both victims, but was also overcome.

■

In Parma, Ohio, 23-year-old Ernest Pesek was dressing up as Dracula for Halloween and wanted to make it look like he had a stake through his heart. He placed a nearly inch-thick board beneath his shirt, then drove a double-edged knife into the board. The board cracked, however, and the knife went into his chest. Pesek died two hours later.

■

Dr. Ely Perlman, New York City's official pollen counter, died of respiratory failure.

■

Eleven-year-old actress Judith Barsi, who played a girl murdered by her father in a 1984 made-for-television movie, *Fatal Vision*, was shot to death by her father, who also killed his wife before taking his own life.

■

In Prague, a woman distraught after learning that her husband had been unfaithful, jumped from a third-story window. She landed on the husband, who was entering the building at that moment. He died; she survived.

■

Marilyn J. McCusker of Osceola Mills, Pennsylvania, who sued the Rushton Mining Company in 1977, charging that sex discrimination kept her from being hired as a miner, as part of her settlement was awarded a job. Two years later, she was killed by falling rocks while working in a mine during a cave-in. No one else was injured.

■

Fumietsu Okubo, 65, of Toyama, Japan, choked to death after becoming entangled in his seat belt in 1986 on the first day of enforcement of Japan's mandatory seat-belt law.

■

JoAnn Miner, food editor of the *Orange County Register* in California, died after choking while eating dinner.

■

Alice Fleetwood, 59, of Seymour, Indiana, a cancer patient at Bartholomew County Hospital, was killed while undergoing radiation therapy when part of a cobalt machine fell on her and fractured her skull.

■

Seven weeks after his father accidentally blew his brains out in 1981 trying to show that guns can be safe, 16-year-old Michael Fredette of Ludlow, Massachusetts, went hunting and was killed by a blast from his own rifle.

■

During the same week in May, 1989 hit-and-run drivers in Washington, D.C., and Oakland Park, Florida, were themselves killed within minutes by other hit-and-run drivers.

Julius McNeil, 29, was at a church in Jackson, Mississippi, waiting to attend his 14-year-old brother's baptism, when he apparently slipped, fell into the pool used for baptism and drowned, according to the police. They said McNeil was alone at the time of the incident.

In Tichigan Lake, Wisconsin, 22-year-old Mary Ann Ashpole and her husband Otto were celebrating Halloween by going from house to house asking for drinks. After one too many, she tripped over a railroad tie used for terracing in a neighbor's yard and fell on her glass, which slashed her throat and killed her.

Sex Is Its Own Punishment

James Ferrozzo, assistant manager of San Francisco's Condor Club, was crushed to death in 1983 when an elevator piano on which he was having sex with the topless club's star stripper rose 12 feet from the floor on an electric pulley and pinned him to the ceiling, crushing his lungs. Police speculated Ferrozzo tripped the switch accidentally during the after-hours affair, but since the piano rises very slowly on the pulley, they were puzzled why the couple didn't simply jump off before it got to the ceiling.

Fire department rescuers spent nearly three hours trying to free the stripper from under the 204-pound Ferrozzo. She sustained only bruises. She told police she had been drinking heavily and remembered little until she woke up on the piano. She could not explain why she was nude.

■

A Silver Spring, Maryland, man contracted rabies after having sex with a raccoon. The man defended himself against animal cruelty charges by pointing out it was already dead when the affair was consummated.

■

In Britain, 60 percent of the women surveyed in a 1987 opinion poll said they preferred to go out to a restaurant for dinner than stay home and have sex.

An emotionally troubled 22-year-old man performed a complicated eight-hour abdominal operation on himself in an effort to reduce his sex drive, according to the *Journal of the American Medical Association*. Using mirrors and professional surgical equipment, the man opened his abdomen and tried to sever the nerves to his adrenal gland, which influences sexual and aggressive feelings. Two months earlier, the man had removed his testicles.

■

When Philadelphia's prison board ordered condoms distributed to convicts to prevent the spread of AIDS, board member M. Mark Mendel, who opposed the distribution program, noted sex between prisoners is illegal and added he doubted that prisoners who rape other inmates would use the condoms.

■

A 20 year-old Akron, Ohio, woman was hospitalized for hypothermia after spending four days underneath a man who died just after they had sex in the front seat of a car. "I just thought he was a hard sleeper," she told her rescuers.

■

The *Texas City Sun* reported in a 1988 crime column that a woman opened her barn to discover one of her horses with its hind legs tied up in the air and a chair behind him.

■

A Detroit jury awarded $1 million to a man who sued a Pepsi-Cola bottler, claiming his transsexualism was triggered by a 1978 collision with a Pepsi truck that injured his head and groin. An appeals court overturned the jury's verdict and approved the bottler's motion for a new trial.

■

Wayne Stanton, administrator of the federal Family Support Administration, proposed solving the problem of teenage pregnancy by detaining teens until 5 p.m. on school days. He cited studies showing many teenage girls become pregnant between 3 p.m. and 5 p.m., when youths are unsupervised at home after school.

■

Transvestite James Kubicek of Olmsted Falls, Ohio, was killed when he tied himself to a railroad track to masturbate and was not able to untie himself before a train came along and hit him.

■

A Norwalk, Connecticut, man won a worker's compensation award after catching AIDS while working in Zaire. He claimed he contracted the condition because of numerous sexual liaisons with local women procured by his employer for its workers.

Injudicious
Judges

Judge Juan Flores sentenced Jose Lopez of Villarcia, Paraguay, to die before a firing squad in 1984 for a shotgun killing, even though it meant that his Siamese twin brother, Alfredo, joined at the side, would die, too, and despite evidence that Alfredo had actually tried to prevent Jose from pulling the trigger.

■

A Minnesota Supreme Court justice was charged with cheating on a 1983 multistate bar exam that he took while trying to qualify to practice law in other states. He was given special permission to take the exam in his office but then admitted to peeking in a book to help him answer a question. He later explained that he thought it was okay to peek during the bar exam.

■

A U.S. magistrate in Los Angeles angered people in 1985 when he released an accused child molester on bail, ruling that the man posed no danger to the community because in his opinion Los Angeles has no community standards on child molesting. His decision was promptly reversed by a federal judge.

■

A Springfield, Massachusetts, Superior Court judge gave a 32-year-old man only a three-year suspended sentence after he had admitted raping his daughter over a period of years. Answering media criticism of the decision, the judge pointed out that his decision also calls for the 650-pound defendant to "stay away" from his daughter and his other five children.

■

An Alabama judge, attending a national conference of family court judges on problems of child abuse was arrested in Providence, Rhode Island, and charged with molesting the 13-year-old grandson of another judge attending the conference.

■

A Colorado judge, filling in for a judge who was ill, sentenced to work-release (part-time jail) a man who pleaded guilty to impersonating a police officer in 1986 in order to strip-search two teenage girls he had encountered. The judge reasoned that the man was a hero because the girls were on a double date with two boys at the time and were down to their underwear. "Thank God he came along when he did," said the judge, "or the consequences could have been much worse."

In 1983, the same judge sentenced a man to work-release even after he had been convicted of shooting his wife to death with five shots to the face and chest, reasoning that she had provoked him by leaving him without warning.

■

A Wisconsin judge sentenced a 25-year-old man to three years' probation for sexual assault on the five-year-old daughter of the man's girlfriend, finding that the girl was "unusually sexually promiscuous" and that the man was "unable" to fend off the girl's advances.

■

A Texas District Court judge sentenced a 31-year-old man to 35 years in prison for stealing a 12-oz., $2 can of Spam in Houston in 1984.

During a 1980 speech to corrections officers, a Colorado judge criticized legislatures for passing laws that require judges to handle nontraditional cases in which they have had little experience. "I'd just love to have a garden-variety rape case," he said. "It keeps you awake in the afternoon and provides a little vicarious pleasure."

A New York City judge ordered a prostitute to be seated next to him at the bench for several hours during court proceedings in 1984. The reason he did this, he said, was "to keep her from sleeping in the courtroom."

A Philadelphia judge removed himself from all future sex-crime cases after making a comment during a 1986 rape trial that the victim was "coyote ugly" and "the ugliest girl I have ever seen in my entire life."

The California Commission on Judicial Qualification charged a Los Angeles Municipal Court judge with misconduct for several incidents. Once, after inviting a lawyer into his chambers, he thrust a personal vibrator against the buttocks of the astonished man; he repeatedly asked a female clerk (a married woman) in open court, "Did you get any last night?"; and he once grabbed another judicial officer by the testicles in open court.

Weird Undertaker Stories

A Brownsville, Texas, family sued a funeral home because employees had dropped the casket during the funeral for a stillborn baby, allowing the body to roll across the floor and come to rest at the feet of the grieving family.

■

Willie M. Stokes, Jr., was buried in Chicago in a special coffin designed to look like a Cadillac Seville, complete with flashing head and tail lights, a steering wheel, and a chrome grill. At Stokes' request, his body lay open in the casket buried in a red velvet suit and fedora, clutching fistfuls of money with fingers filled with diamond rings. A funeral home operator described Stokes as "very car-conscious."

■

In Palermo, Italy, the funeral of Antonio Percelli was halted when Percelli, mistakenly declared dead, climbed out of the casket. Percelli's move so startled his mother that she died on the spot of a heart attack, and was buried later at the gravesite that had been ordered for Percelli.

■

Invesigators in Jacksonville, Florida, found 44 decomposing bodies stacked like cordwood in a funeral home closet in 1988. Lewis J. Howell, owner of the Howell mortuary, allegedly attributed the delay in burying the bodies to paperwork problems rather than any intention to cut expenses. Most bodies were recent deaths, but one certificate indicated that death occurred in 1978.

■

A New Jersey police chief was accused of ordering the opening of a grave because he had realized that he had loaned the grieving family a hat for the casket-viewing but had not gotten it back after the funeral.

■

A 23-year-old woman confessed to having had sex with as many as 40 corpses in the late 1970s while working at a Sacramento mortuary. She was apprehended when police found her naked in the back of a hearse with the casket open. The family of one of the dead people sued her and the mortuary and won $142,500.

■

A funeral home director in Wagoner, Oklahoma, was sued for $975,000 in 1982 after the parents of a dead girl found a human foot inside a bag that was supposed to contain the child's papers and belongings. The director said the incident was "an honest mistake blown out of proportion."

■

A New York City woman sued a funeral home for $10 million for the shock and emotional distress she received upon viewing the body of her 6'2" husband crammed into an undersized casket at a funeral home. According to court papers, her husband's body had to be bent to get it into the casket, making him look "as if his neck had been broken."

Jealous Rages

A California woman was awarded $6 million by a jury in 1987 from her ex-husband, a gynecologist. He and an associate were found to have sewn shut her vagina (during an intended hysterectomy) because he was angry that his wife had had an affair. The two doctors testified at the trial that any mistakes they had made in the 1984 operation were "not intentional."

■

Walter Davis, 75, was found not guilty by reason of insanity in 1986 in the murder of his wife. According to testimony, she had harangued him for five hours one day about a conversation he had had, in her presence, with a woman in a grocery store on how to preserve unused portions of a loaf of bread.

■

In Sao Paulo, Brazil, a husband, discovering his wife with another man, glued her hand to the lover's penis with acrylic cement. Despite successful surgery to separate the body parts, the man died several days later of toxic poisoning from the cement's being absorbed into the bloodstream.

■

An 84-year-old woman shot her 81-year-old husband in the leg with a .38-calibre revolver during an argument over her having kissed a pastor after church. "I tried to tell him it was in the Bible, but he kept pushing me and yelling," she told police, who charged her with assault with a deadly weapon.

A Maryland man reached a settlement in his lawsuit against his girlfriend in Bradenton, Florida. He had charged in the lawsuit that she had bitten off chunks of his tongue so that "no other woman would want him," according to court papers.

A Tennessee woman of 43 married her son, 26, in 1978, keeping secret for six years the fact that she was his mother because she did not want any other woman to have him. She had given him up for adoption at age 3, then had formally adopted him (along with her ex-husband) after the marriage. The son believed that the adoption was merely a name change; he separated from her immediately upon learning the facts.

Bangkae, Thailand, police arrested an 18-year-old woman, charging her with cutting off her husband's penis while he slept, in retaliation for an alleged extramarital affair. After a neighbor had brought the screaming man to a hospital, the doctor advised him to return and find the penis, which the wife had tossed out the window. The neighbor returned just in time to retrieve it from a covey of ducks.

A 91-year-old woman sued her 79-year-old husband of 53 years for divorce in Queens, New York, accusing him of having had an affair with a "younger woman," age 70. According to the lawsuit, her husband admitted to having been seeing the other woman for 40 years, and she decided to leave when he became abusive and threatened to hit her with his cane. As the moving van pulled up to the house to take away her belongings, all her husband could say was, "Did you wash my clothes?"

In Los Angeles, a 26-year-old man was sentenced to one month in jail in 1988 for killing his wife's six-week-old kitten by cooking it in a microwave oven because the wife had gone to a movie with a friend.

In an attempt to make her husband jealous, a Dayton, Ohio, woman wrote a love note to one of his friends in which she described a fictitious affair with the friend. "Your kisses are better than his, I've liked you from the first time I laid eyes on you," she wrote in the note. Her husband allegedly lured the friend to their house and beat him with a pipe. "I knew that it (the note) would make him jealous, but he just went nuts," she said. She also noted that on a previous occasion he had written a letter concerning a fictitious affair of his own.

Weird Clergy

 B uddhist priests blessed 200,000 used brassieres in a temple memorial service for cast-off underwear in Tokyo.

■

 I n 1985 a Catholic priest was arrested in Port Richey, Florida, and charged with shoplifting a package of condoms from a drug store.

■

 T he founder of a fundamentalist Christian community near Petersburg, Virginia, was convicted of manslaughter, along with the parents of a 2-year-old boy, after the boy died in 1982 as a result of two hours of paddling that she said was necessary to win a "test of wills" with the child.

■

 A n award of $1.8 million was made in a lawsuit against the Catholic Church—bringing to about $10 million the amount the Church has had to pay out for failing to prevent child molesting by a single priest in New Orleans. The priest is serving 20 years in prison for molesting 36 boys.

■

 A California woman sued a Roman Catholic archdiocese for $21 million because she said the father of her child is a priest in the archdiocese. Further, she asked the court to determine officially which of two priests is the actual father, she having narrowed down to two from the seven priests she claimed to have had sex with. She claims both potential fathers had had sex with her in the rectory of the church on the same day. She said she had wanted to become a nun, then "lost faith in the church."

■

Rev. Jim Brown of Ironton, Ohio, told the First Church of Nazarene congregation in 1986 that the theme song to the old TV show, "Mr. Ed," played in reverse, contains satanic messages. According to Brown, "A horse is a horse, of course, of course," backwards, is "the source is satan."

■

A Bangor, Maine, minister, head of the state Moral Majority chapter, resigned amid allegations of his having had sex with his church organist.

■

A minister in Three Rivers, Michigan, spearheaded an anti-homosexual drive after a career in the 1970s as a female impersonator working gay bars in Detroit. He once appeared as "Patty" in an Andrews Sisters imitation and another time danced in a red afro wig under the name Terrell Grant. At the time of his religious conversion, he sported a light-red pompadour, a stiff, brushy moustache, and long, feathery sideburns.

■

In England, Canon Michael Dittmer, who believes in "balance" in funeral eulogies, described Fred Clark, 52, as a "very disagreeable man with little good in him who would not be missed." Dittmer later apologized.

Sixty residents of the Seminole Health Club nudist camp near Miami comprise a Christian mission that worships twice a week in the nude. According to leader Elijah Jackson, "We're not trying to start a cult here, but I think nudity adds something to Christianity."

Unusual Weapons

In Bloomington, Indiana, a 41-year-old woman was convicted of murdering her boyfriend by repeatedly dropping a 14-lb. bowling ball on his head as he lay watching TV on the floor of the apartment they shared.

■

A man was charged with manslaughter by police in Huntsville, Alabama, when the woman who was performing fellatio on him choked to death. He claimed the death was accidental. According to his attorney, "It was an oral sex act, and the girl died. Well, what is his crime?" A grand jury later decided not to indict.

■

In 1978 a Paris grocer stabbed his wife to death with a wedge of Parmesan cheese.

■

In 1984 a New Zealand man killed his wife by stabbing her repeatedly in the stomach with a frozen sausage.

■

A Louisville woman pleaded guilty to adding powerful laxatives to her husband's vitamin capsules every day for three months in order to make him ill so that his family would offer him financial assistance on the couple's overdue mortgage payments.

■

In Bedford, Texas, a 16-year-old boy and two companions held up a 7-Eleven in 1984, brandishing only a snake. They made off with three six-packs of beer as the clerk wrestled with the biting but nonpoisonous garter snake the youths tossed at him.

■

A 32-year-old Woodbury, New Jersey, man pleaded guilty to aggravated assault and animal cruelty in 1986 after an argument with his girlfriend in which he tried to stuff pieces of her pet iguana, Abraham, down her throat.

■

A 52-year-old woman in Albany, New York, successfully warded off a young man intent on taking her purse, striking him repeatedly with a hot fudge sundae she had just purchased at an ice-cream parlor.

■

In East Naples, Florida, a would-be robber became so angry at learning that his amputee-victim was not carrying drugs that he beat the man on the head with the man's artificial leg.

■

Police in Tacoma, Washington, jailed a man on Thanksgiving day in 1987 for assaulting his girlfriend with the 21-lb. turkey they were baking.

■

In Birmingham, Alabama, a man was convicted of assault and battery after hitting his wife over the head repeatedly with their 1½-lb. chihuahua during a domestic dispute.

Weirdos in Training

A 15-year-old boy in Grosse Pointe Woods, Michigan, pulled a gun on an orthodontist and demanded that he remove the braces on his teeth. The boy told the doctor, who was not the one who had put the braces on, that he didn't care about going to jail "as long as I can have my bands off." The doctor called police, then stalled until they arrived. Police eventually disarmed the boy after a struggle in which two shots were fired.

■

In 1983 it was reported that kids in New York City were stealing subway tokens by sucking them out of turnstile slots, a distance of about two inches, where the token remains until the subway patron has gone completely through the turnstile. According to a Transit Authority official, some kids were making $50 to $100 a day.

■

In Beckley, West Virginia, a woman was beaten by a mob of sixth graders in 1987 when she visited her son's school dressed as a "Care Bear" on Valentine's Day.

■

Hal Warden, 12, married Wendy Chappell, 14, in Nashville but was divorced a month later as she claimed he "was acting like a 10-year-old." Hal, who was working construction at the time, was ordered to pay $30 a week to support their child; however, in a case that went all the way to the Tennessee Court of Appeals, the amount was reduced to $15 a week (the entire amount of Hal's allowance from his parents) when he quit to return to 7th grade. At 14, Hal married Catherine Trent, 15, but they divorced shortly after their daughter, Ashley, was born; Hal and Catherine had worked out a 50-50 split of Ashley's support.

■

In Chesapeake, Virginia, in 1985, William V. Scott, 4, eluded police at speeds of up to 35 mph on his $900, 110-lb. motorized tricycle before he was apprehended. J. M. Liptrap, the arresting officer, commented, "William can fly on that little thing. If he sees a police car, he just automatically takes off. All you can do is follow and hope he slows down."

■

Kerry Shea, 14, "just lost control" of her toothbrush, and swallowed it, but it was retrieved shortly afterward by a DePere, Wisconsin, doctor. Shea offered only that she was "brushing the back of my tongue because I saw on TV that it helps to get a lot of sugar that way" when "it just slipped and I swallowed it."

■

In an affidavit in a 1987 Salt Lake City case, one of the teenage kidnapers of the son of a millionaire businessman said he passed the idle time waiting for the ransom money to be delivered by doing his homework.

■

In 1987, two seventh-grade girls in Roy, Utah, interested a manufacturer in "Easy-Off Underwear"—side-opening bras and underpants fastened with Velcro. One was quoted in explanation, "Like when you're in gym, while you have to hold the

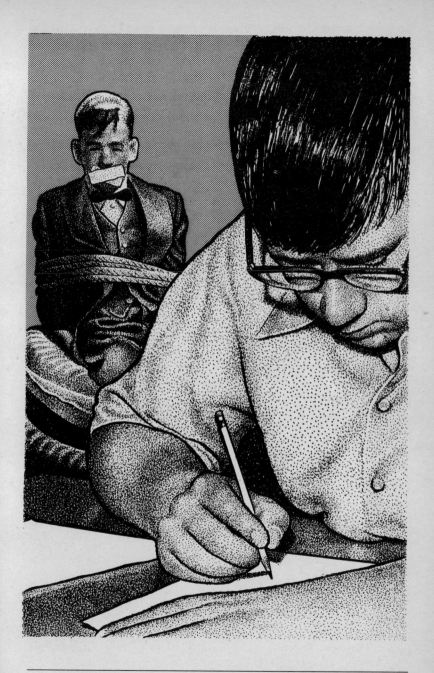

towel while you're taking off your bra and your underwear, and your main problem is you're afraid you're going to fall down or drop your towel."

■

The Oakland Beach Elementary School principal in Warwick, Rhode Island, had to segregate boys and girls at recess to protect the boys. The girls were enjoying a fad of terrorizing boys by pulling their hair and kicking them in the shins and testicles.

■

In a 1987 poll asking South Korean children to name their favorite things, the children ranked their mothers first but put their fathers third—behind a serving of beef.

■

In Houston in 1987, a 10-year-old boy shot and killed his father, Edward Simon, 45, and wounded his mother, Mary Simon, 47, with a .38-calibre revolver when they refused to let him go outside and play.

Weird Pieces
of Legislation

In 1987 Rep. Will Green Poindexter introduced a bill in the Mississippi legislature to permit dwarfs to hunt deer with crossbows during archery season.

■

An Alaskan assemblyman introduced a bill to punish "public flatulence, crepitation, gaseous emission, and miasmic effluence," carrying a penalty of $100.

■

Sen. Matthew Feldman introduced a bill into the New Jersey Senate to allow a $1,000 fine and six months in jail for anyone who profits by guaranteeing a "curse" on a person's enemy through the use of, for example, the "evil eye," demons, voodoo, "bones" or pronouncing magic words of the occult designed to bring bad luck.

■

The Chico, California, City Council enacted a ban on nuclear weapons, setting a $500 fine for anyone detonating one within the city limits.

■

The Wyoming legislature in 1980 banned the photographing of rabbits from January through April without an official permit.

Rep. George Beard of Culpepper, Virginia, introduced a bill in the state house to prevent dead bodies from being kept in places where food is served.

In 1984, Missouri state Rep. Fred Williams introduced a bill to prohibit nose-blowing in restaurants if done in a "loud, obnoxious, or offensive manner," and carrying a $200 fine. Williams cited numerous encounters with nose-blowers in restaurants, especially at breakfast, along with many constituent complaints, as provoking his bill. "I've had to get out of a restaurant to keep from throwing up," he said.

In 1987, Philadelphia Councilman John F. Street introduced a bill to ban people from carrying snakes on public streets, sidewalks, and parks and in recreation areas. Street told the *Philadelphia Inquirer* that the bill was needed because he was "tired" of seeing people carrying snakes in public.

A 1982 city ordinance in Kennesaw, Georgia (24 miles north of Atlanta), requires every able-bodied resident to have a gun and ammunition. About nine of ten Kennesaw households had guns before the ordinance was passed. In nearby Acworth, Georgia, the city council responded by passing an ordinance requiring all households to own fishing poles.

Texas State Rep. Jim Kaster introduced a bill requiring anyone who intends to commit a crime to notify the future victim at least 24 hours in advance, orally or in writing, and to notify victims of their right to use deadly force to resist certain crimes.

The Winchester (Indiana) City Council passed an antipornography ordinance, which, according to state law, must be published in a local newspaper before it is allowed to take effect. However, the local newspaper refused to print it because the wording was "obscene."

■

Oklahoma State Rep. Cleta Deatherage introduced a bill to require men to obtain advance written permission from any female with whom they engage in sexual intercourse. The man must also warn the female that she could become pregnant as a result and that childbirth could be hazardous to her health. If the female cannot read a written statement, the warnings must be read to her in her native language. The bill was defeated.

■

Alaska State Sen. Bob Ziegler introduced a bill to make it illegal for a dog to impersonate a police dog. No dog other than a police dog could use police-dog facilities, eat police-dog food, bite criminals, or loiter in the vicinity of a fire hydrant.

Products of Free Enterprise

Two Soviet inventors, I. Bogomolova and S. Kimaikin, requested a patent in 1986 for an edible vodka bottle that, when digested, reduces the blood-alcohol level in the body.

■

Lore Harp of San Mateo, California, introduced La Funelle, a disposable paper funnel that permits women to urinate while standing up.

■

Le Chien, a New York City pet salon, marketed perfumes for dogs, including Martine, at $38 for 3.3 ounces in a crystal sprayer, and Christophe for the male, at $30.

■

A California firm markets solar-powered tombstones that talk back to graveside visitors with recorded messages that play perpetually.

■

A Tokyo firm named Jippo runs a mobile pet funeral service. Employees in shocking-pink jumpsuits, in a van decorated with a green-pasture, blue-sky motif, make house calls on grieving pet owners to perform a five-minute ceremony consisting of placing the pet's remains in a coffin, reading poetry, cremating the animal, and giving the owner the ashes in an urn—all for $400.

■

Willie Holmes of Hillsborough, California, developed a snorkel and tube for guests in high-rise buildings in which fires break out. Using the snorkel, guests could reach down through the toilet trap to the water line in the tank to use the oxygen in the air vent that runs to the roof until they could be rescued.

■

Public toilets built in some European cities in the 1980s featured automatic lights, air conditioning, disco music, paper dispensers, perfumed disinfectants, and stall doors that open automatically every 15 minutes to discourage overuse.

■

At a California Energy Commission symposium in Fresno in 1980, a Holstein cow was milked by a professional milk machine powered by gas produced from her own manure. A Commission spokesman told dairy farmers, "Not only will you be exporting milk to the city of the future, you will be exporting electricity as well—electricity generated from . . . manure."

■

Frank O. Hill of Union, South Carolina, manufactures jewelry from quail droppings. He said he was a quail breeder ready to close his business in the 1970s when he noticed "how beautiful a quail dropping is" and embedded one in clear plastic to make a tie tack. "I found that I could sell a quail egg for a dime, but a quail only laid one egg a day. However, I could sell the dropping in plastic for $5, and a quail produces about 40 droppings a day."

■

Seattle designer Paul Willms crafted a line of beachwear in 1987 from the skins of butterfly fish, grouper, and other fish, charging $950 for a bikini.

■

A Richland, Washington, inventor produced a hand-held gizmo whose only function is to select numbers at random to play in state lottery contests. Its marketing makes no claim about winning combinations but rather emphasizes the reduction of mental strain in trying to come up with combinations.

■

In 1980, former British army Sgt. Bob Acraman opened a vacation camp where visitors could spend three days in an imitation Nazi prison camp. "They'll have a horrible time and love every minute of it," he said. "There are plenty of crazy people around . . . who love being locked up and made to suffer behind barbed wire." Scheduled were 2 a.m. searches, prison meals, and psychological interrogation for those who try to escape.

■

Among the items at a 1987 Japanese inventors' fair was "six-day underwear"—a garment with three leg holes and instructions for the user to rotate it 120 degrees each day for three days and then turn it inside out for another three days.

■

A gadget that detects urine was put into service in Singapore in 1987 to stem an outbreak of people urinating in elevators. When a sensor detects urine, it jams the elevator and activates a video camera.

■

A New York outfit called Animal Manors, Inc., will construct a doghouse that is an exact replica of the owner's house for $10,000 plus options.

■

A London bill-collection agency, Smelly Tramps, Ltd., duns deadbeats by sending foul-smelling vagabonds to sit in the debtor's office until he agrees to pay up. The firm, which uses a special "stomach-churning" chemical that makes the office virtually uninhabitable within 10 minutes, claims a 90% success rate.

■

To curb rising water bills, Japanese National Railways installed "intelligent toilets" to regulate the amount of water used by patrons, but that led users to wonder whether enough water was passing through the toilet when flushed. Another Japanese railway went a step further than JNR: It attached an electronic device that broadcasts the sound of massive amounts of flushing water, so that customers no longer worry about hygiene.

Spectacular Suicide Attempts

Remorseful after killing his girlfriend in October 1983, a man tried unsuccessfully to commit suicide several times. At a roadside park in Mississippi, he tried to cut his wrist, but later reported that it hurt too much. In Miami, he intended to drown himself but found the water too cold. While driving around in his pickup truck, he tried to poison himself by eating rancid chicken, and also tried chainsmoking two packs of cigarettes before abandoning the attempts and turning himself in to police in Houston, where he was eventually sentenced to 15 years for the slaying.

■

The *British Journal of Psychiatry* reported in 1988 that a Canadian teenager who shot himself in the mouth in a suicide attempt three years earlier had actually torn apart the section of his brain responsible for his remarkable compulsion to wash his hands as many as 100 times a day—a compulsion that had led to his suicide attempt in the first place. The boy survived, is much improved, and saw his IQ rise to its pre-illness level.

■

Nino Placenza, 75, tried to kill himself in Bradenton, Florida, in 1983, by drilling a hole in his head with a power drill, but only wound up in intensive care.

■

Mohammed Abdel Rahman, 29, leaped to his death from the balcony of his hotel on his wedding night in Cairo in 1987 after he discovered that his mother-in-law tricked him into marrying the uglier of her two daughters. Rahman had entrusted wedding details to the mother-in-law when he was sent out of the country on business shortly before the wedding, and she slipped the other daughter's name onto the dotted line.

■

Doris Kennedy, 38 weeks pregnant, hanged herself to death in her London apartment in 1985 because of depression resulting from construction delays to the new baby's bathroom.

■

A London man survived successive suicide attempts that involved driving his car head-on at 70 mph into a bridge embankment and then climbing a pole and grabbing a 132,000-volt power line.

■

Another Briton, from Taunton, failed in seven attempts to kill himself after breaking up with his girlfriend in 1987. He threw himself at a total of four cars and one truck, jumped out of a window, and tried to strangle himself. One of the car drivers suffered a heart attack, and two policemen were injured trying to restrain the man.

■

Roh Ki-hwa, 34, a Seoul housewife, hanged herself to death in 1987 because she was embarrassed at her failure to prepare her husband's lunch on schedule during a company picnic. She had forgotten to set her watch ahead one hour for the May 10 changeover to daylight savings time, Korea's first such changeover in 25 years, and was thus one hour late in making the meal.

A 25-year-old man, who intended to commit suicide earlier in the year on the Berkeley, California, pier but had mistakenly fallen asleep, tried again, intending to leap from the Golden Gate Bridge. However, he had thought the drop would be painful so he consumed a large amount of drugs just before climbing down on a girder for his final fall. He was rescued by a bridge painter while hanging from the girder, explaining that he was waiting for the drugs to kick in before he would let go.

■

A 38-year-old Orland Park, Illinois, man, distraught over an argument with his girlfriend about buying drapes, killed himself by cutting a hole in his waterbed, sticking his head through it and drowning himself.

■

Yoshio Miyauchi, a Tokyo high-school baseball coach, immolated himself on New Year's Eve in 1981 following a team argument over the dangers of smoking.

■

A Lincoln, Nebraska, man was unsuccessful in his suicide attempt. He had dropped, respectively, a telephone, a radio, an electric fan, and a toaster into his bathtub while bathing.

■

A 17-year-old bodybuilder leaped 135 feet from the San Mateo Bridge in California, intending to commit suicide, but when the leap failed to kill him, he swam a half mile to an embankment, fell asleep, then woke the next morning and climbed a maintenance ladder under the bridge back to retrieve his truck, which had just been towed away in preparation for rush-hour traffic.

■

A man, about 35 years old but carrying no identification, shopping at a Phoenix pawn shop, asked the clerk if he could plug in a 10″ circular saw to test it before purchasing it, then committed suicide by practically cutting his head off.

■

Texas fisherman Danny Ray Davis killed himself with a shotgun blast the day before he was scheduled to appear before a grand jury investigating allegations of cheating at bass-fishing tournaments.

From the Police Blotter

Patrolman Robert D'Ascanio of Pittsfield, Massachusetts, apprehended a purse-snatcher he was about to lose one night by barking like a dog and then shouting, "Okay, let the dog loose." That caused the suspect to stop in his tracks. The Pittsfield police department had eliminated its K-9 unit (consisting of one dog) three years before.

■

In 1982 Clearwater, Florida, police arrested a 33-year-old man for prowling around a neighborhood near the motel at which he was staying after they received complaints from four people that he had knocked on their doors at night asking for Vaseline for his hemorrhoids.

■

"Hero," Tom and Priscilla Nelson's burglar-scaring robot, which cost Nelson $1,500 and 250 hours' work to make, was stolen from the Nelsons' Arlington, Virginia, home while they were on vacation. Hero, who had been programed to tell burglars that he had just called police, was later found in Washington, D.C., in the backseat of a stolen car, partly disassembled and with dead batteries.

■

Police in Key West, Florida, arrested a 20-year-old man after discovering him "extremely intoxicated" on a street. He was "covered literally from head to toe" with white specks, said the police, and when a subsequent search turned up plastic bags containing dried-out typewriter correcting fluid bottles, the man confessed that he was addicted to it.

■

A 30-year-old man was arrested in Glen Ellyn, Illinois, and charged with terrorizing women in the University of Illinois area during most of the 1970s as the the "enema bandit." Allegedly, he would break into apartments and rob people, but when the victim was a woman, he would also give her an enema.

■

A three-hundred-fifty-pound man attempted to rob a Long Island jeweler with a gun, but before the loot was handed to him, he tripped and fell and was unable to get back to his feet before the police arrived.

■

A Houston man was fined $10,000 and placed on ten years' probation in 1987 for stealing nearly 80,000 rolls of toilet paper from Jefferson Davis Hospital. He said he was the victim of a record-keeping error.

■

In Canadaigua, New York, a 39-year-old man was indicted on 1,822 sexual assault charges—all involving the same victim, whom he allegedly assaulted nearly every day for five years. Prosecutors said the number of counts against one victim may be a national record.

■

Two men with guns fired a total of twelve shots at each other at point-blank range in a Cleveland apartment in 1984, but no one was injured. Police speculated that the men, aged 76

and 77, missed because one had glaucoma and the other had to prop himself up with a cane each time before firing.

■

São Paolo police caught two elderly burglars redhanded during a 1984 break-in because, according to an inspector, one's voice was faltering because of his age and the other was hard of hearing. The inspector said one, who was 74, "just took his time and kept up his leisurely pace. He was still busy stealing when we arrived. [The other man] tried to escape but his varicose veins slowed him down."

■

Security officers at Forbes Field near Topeka, Kansas, were forced to shoot two dogs who were mating on a runway in 1987 shortly before President Reagan's plane was scheduled to land. The officers said the dogs, which resisted earlier attempts by security officers to uncouple them, posed a danger to Reagan's plane.

M̲esquite, Texas, police broke up a hammer and tire-iron fight between two women at a truck stop. The two had been arguing on their CB radios as to which of them had bigger breasts and had agreed to meet at the truck stop to compare bosoms.

■

S̲heriff's deputies on a stakeout in Gainesville, Florida, diligently watched, for 17 consecutive days, a motorcycle they had planted as a target in hopes of catching an elusive burglar, but during one officer's two-minute restroom break, the cycle was stolen.

■

A̲ man locked up in the Cook County (Illinois) jail on murder charges escaped in 1988 by getting the drop on guards using a "gun" carved out of a soap bar.

■

I̲ndianapolis police officer Timothy Day had to be hospitalized when a gust of wind blew into his face the contents of a sack of cocaine he had seized as evidence.

■

I̲n Los Angeles a man mugged Mrs. Hollis Sharpe while she was walking her poodle, Jonathan, on a nightly stroll. She was thrown to the ground, and the mugger made off with the handbag Mrs. Sharpe was carrying—which contained nothing except a plastic bag she had just used to scoop up after Jonathan.

■

A̲ 22-year-old man was robbed on a Yonkers, New York, street while he was dressed as a woman. According to police, the victim initially yielded $10 to the robbers, but one became angry and reached into the victim's bra, where he found another $20. Police approached and the two robbers fled, but one of them was captured when he ran into a street sign and collapsed.

■

In Wichita, Kansas, a man was charged with assault and battery on his girlfriend, stemming, according to police, from her inability to buy a winning lottery ticket. As police officer Jim Whittredge explained, "Every time she scratched a losing ticket, the guy smacked her, and she lost five times."

■

A Cleveland State University anatomy professor pleaded guilty to manslaughter in the death of his wife. According to police, she had been suspended, nude, from a third-floor window of the couple's Cleveland Heights home by a rope tied to her ankle, as preparation for a sex act, when the husband lost control of the rope.

■

In Hong Kong a young man was arrested for being a Peeping Tom after he had fallen 12 floors onto a canopy. According to police, he was looking into the apartment of a 50-year-old woman on the 12th floor while hanging naked by one hand from a ledge and "performing an indecent" with the other hand. When the woman saw him and screamed, he tried to scramble back to the roof where he had left his clothes, but he lost his grip.

■

Atlanta, Georgia, police arrested a 34-year-old, 5'1", 350 pound woman for selling drugs. A subsequent search turned up a pistol completely hidden under her left breast and $2,000 in cash completely hidden in a crease in her abdomen.

■

Wythe County (Virginia) Circuit Court judge Willis Wood pleaded guilty to driving under the influence of alcohol after he was apprehended on his way to a meeting at an alcohol treatment program.

■

Sheriff's officers near St. Petersburg, Florida, investigated but did not arrest a 79-year-old man who had knocked himself unconscious by administering an electrical shock with a device consisting of a radio transmitter (with Morse Code key), a rheostat set at 12 volts, and an earphone jack—all connected to his penis.

■

A bus carrying five passengers was hit by a car in St. Louis, but by the time police arrived on the scene, fourteen pedestrians had boarded the bus and had begun to complain of whiplash injuries.

■

In Hudiksvall, Sweden, police arrested a 31-year-old father, charging him with stealing $6 from his 3-year-old son's piggy bank.

■

St. Louis police said a Bridgeton, Missouri, man cut the hair of as many as 100 young men, promising them as much as $1,800 and a chance to act in a military recruiting movie if they would sit for the haircuts. According to the Missouri Attorney General's office, no one was ever paid, and no reason was given why the man wanted the haircuts done.

■

When Donald McGarity was run over by an unidentified driver in the Sacramento, California, area, highway patrol officers arriving on the scene found McGarity's hand locked in a "derogatory" hand gesture. According to the coroner, McGarity's spinal column was severed by the collision, thus causing the body to freeze into the position it assumed when hit.

■

Near Pine Ridge Village in South Dakota, a Sioux named Warrior was sentenced to six months in prison for assaulting another Indian, Bruce Pipe on Head, by hitting him on the head with a pipe. Warrior was found guilty of a second count, also—hitting Pipe on Head on the arm with a pipe.

Weird TV and Radio

Eddie Seidel, 15, leaped off a bridge to his death in St. Paul because he was despondent over the cancellation of the TV series *Battlestar Galactica*.

■

Fire crews responding to a call in Smethwick, England, found George Thurlow standing at a door waving furiously. He directed firefighters upstairs to a back bedroom, where they found, in thick smoke, Thurlow's wife and two elderly daughters sitting calmly in the burning room, watching the American TV show *St. Elsewhere*. One daughter was smoking a cigarette.

■

When the New England Telephone Company in Providence called a news conference to announce that its new directory would be in four columns instead of five, two TV stations showed up with full camera crews to cover it.

■

A Riverdale, Illinois, resident was charged with shooting his 88-year-old mother because she insisted on watching *Cosby* while he preferred another show.

■

A 47-year-old woman, described as "large," was convicted of shoplifting items, including a $695 color TV set and fur coats, that she concealed between her legs as she walked from stores. According to court testimony, the TV set was balanced between her knees, and when she bent over to pick something up, a store employee saw the outline of the TV set under her dress.

■

A London man was charged with kidnaping an exotic dancer when he brought her to his home and forced her to watch an episode of *Dynasty* while topless.

■

When a 28-year-old Philadelphia resident was arrested for murdering his wife in 1981, he explained that she had been practicing witchcraft on him and offered as evidence the fact that he had become inexplicably inspired to watch "boring television shows" such as *Nova* and *Masterpiece Theatre*.

Least Justifiable Homicides

A Parisian nightwatch-man killed his second wife in 1972 because, police theorized, she had overcooked a roast. Seventeen years earlier he had killed his first wife because she had undercooked a meal.

■

In Chicago in 1988, a 24-year-old father was accused of beating his 5-year-old stepson to death when the child, reciting the alphabet, repeatedly was unable to get past "G."

■

A New York City investment broker was convicted of second-degree murder in 1984 for shooting to death the motorist who dented a fender of his $70,000 Ferrari.

■

A London man was accused of strangling his wife to death because she put a pot of mustard and a newspaper on the wrong side of the plate at dinner.

■

In Washington, D.C., a woman was charged with stabbing her sister to death in 1986 during a quarrel over the sister's having prepared too many potatoes for a meal.

A man in a bar in Fontana, California, shot his estranged wife to death on Valentine's Day in 1982 in an argument over an Indian-head penny.

A St. Louis man was charged with killing his brother in 1986 because the brother had used six rolls of toilet paper from the eight-pack the man had bought only two days before.

A 17-year-old man in Waterbury, Connecticut, was charged with stabbing Elgin Yates to death in 1986. Yates had become aggressive when the charged man had bragged that he looked better in women's clothing than did Yates's girlfriend.

A Forth Worth jury convicted a man in 1981 of shooting a friend to death with a high-caliber rifle during an argument over whether the Tampa Bay Buccaneers had made the National Football League playoffs in 1979. The year before, in Houston, an osteopath was accused of killing his son with a gun during an argument about the recent firing of Houston Oiler coach Bum Phillips and the demand of running back Earl Campbell to be traded.

A 22-year-old student was convicted of murdering a night watchman in a Munich military academy in 1986 so that he could get an advance look at military academy exam questions. He had denied the charges, claiming that he had been on maneuvers with a secret right-wing group when the crime occurred.

Lawrence Timmons, 41, was killed by a Whataburger chef in 1986 in Fort Worth after he had become belligerent about the restaurant's having run out of large hamburger buns.

Inappropriate Uses for Food

A Harrisville, West Virginia, man was found not guilty in the 1985 murder of a local funeral director whom he had stabbed 13 times after awakening to find him licking mayonnaise, ketchup, mustard, and pickle juice (which the licker had spread on the victim's body while he was asleep) off his nude body. A court found that the killer was temporarily insane because of the circumstances.

■

Two Los Angeles bus drivers, one male and one female, reported to police that they were robbed and that the woman was tied up and had had tartar sauce smeared over her body.

■

In Virginia Beach, Virginia, an intruder smeared vanilla and chocolate icing on Robin Graham's sleeping body and in her hair. When she awoke abruptly, the intruder (who had taken the icing from cans in the woman's kitchen) said, "See what happens when you leave your doors unlocked," and fled. She said she did not get a good look at the man because her eyes were pasted shut with icing.

■

A 23-year-old geology major at the University of Southwestern Louisiana failed halfway through his attempt to spend 34 hours seated in a tub of ketchup.

■

A man was arrested in Hammond, Indiana, in 1987 and charged with arson after police were called to his burning home to find him seated in his bathtub covered with butter. After the fire was put out, he resisted arrest, and police found it difficult to hold him because of the butter.

■

In 1980, three sisters in Lansing, Michigan, "got filled with the Holy Spirit" after reading the Bible, according to one, and were arrested shortly afterward riding naked, smeared with mustard, in a stolen truck. In an interview with Associated Press, one sister said the cause was "maybe . . . a little of both [God and the devil] trying to outdo the other."

■

A New York college professor walked into a Dover, New Jersey, 7-Eleven in 1977, stripped naked, and poured ice cream and coffee grounds over his body.

■

A 21-year-old man was charged with public indecency after allegedly placing his penis in a jar of coleslaw dressing at a K-Mart in Downers Grove, Illinois.

■

Two California women, Judy Schwartz and Rickey Berkowitz, were shipwrecked in the Java Sea in 1985. For three weeks, they lived on nothing but toothpaste. After their rescue, Colgate-Palmolive gave them 400 tubes of its toothpaste.

To dramatize the plight of hungry people in Ethiopia, a Mechanics-burg, Pennsylvania, man spent six days in 1988 sitting in a bathtub filled with baked beans and sauce.

Least Competent Criminals

A robbery suspect was arrested after reportedly removing his mask during a holdup at his former place of employment in Newark, New Jersey, in 1987. When he approached an employee and asked for the firm's money, the victim recognized his voice and said, "Dollar Bill, is that you?" The robber then removed his mask and asked, "How did you know it was me?"

■

Five teenagers who vandalized Lincoln's tomb in 1987 were arrested after police saw that they had spray-painted their names on the monument. The five also painted racist slogans and symbols on the tomb and told police that they did it out of boredom.

■

A Washington, D.C., man was indicted by a federal grand jury in 1975 on charges of committing five bank robberies. A common link in three of the robberies was his poor spelling in a note which he handed to the tellers, telling them to put the money in the bag and that he meant "no bullshirt."

■

A man entered the Union Commerce Bank in Cleveland in 1986 and demanded that a teller open the vault. When she explained that the vault would not open because it worked on a timer, he demanded the keys of all the tellers. Then he changed his mind and ran. After he stood pushing the front door of the bank for several seconds, someone yelled "Pull!" and he escaped.

■

Two Colombian cocaine dealers attempting to service a Hackensack, New Jersey, disc-jockey customer, walked into a building with a large antenna on the roof and tried to sell a kilo for $34,000. The building was headquarters of the New Jersey State Police.

■

A Santa Ana, California, man broke his leg and arm when a safe that he was allegedly trying to steal fell on him. After unbolting the safe from the second floor of a pool supply company, he was taking it down a flight of stairs on a hand dolly "when it got away from him, and it went all the way to the bottom, breaking the stairs," said a policeman. The injured man crawled down the stairs and about 150 yards from the scene of the crime, where he was found lying in a gutter and calling for help. He at first claimed to be the victim of a hit-and-run accident, but police said that "the injuries were inconsistent with his story."

■

In 1986 a man fainted while trying to rob the Lafayette Cooperative Bank in Swansea, Massachusetts, with a toy pistol. He had also locked the keys inside his getaway car.

■

A convict broke out of jail in Washington, D.C., then a few days later accompanied his girlfriend to her trial for robbery. At lunch, he went out for sandwiches. She needed to see him and thus had him paged. Police officers recognized his name over the public address system. As he alighted in front of the court house in a car he had stolen during lunch hour, he was arrested.

A robbery suspect was arrested after returning to the same bank he had robbed two days earlier to inquire about opening a savings account there. The man spoke to a teller at First Federal of Champaign, Illinois, two days after the same woman was held up by an armed man. "She recognized him right away," said a police detective.

In Harrieta, Michigan, a 30-year-old man entered a Methodist church on Sunday morning and held the congregation hostage with a rifle. While police were en route, one parishioner asked how much the gun cost; he said $500. Another offered him $500 for it, and he accepted. The hostages took up a collection for the $500, he handed the rifle over, and the police arrested him.

In Mount Vernon, Washington, a young man in green fatigue pants and a baseball cap, wearing a bandana over his face, walked into the Edgewater Tavern on a Thursday evening with a gun and announced a holdup. Because of his high, quivering voice, a couple of the customers started to giggle, and soon everyone in the bar was laughing. The boy fled without any money.

A bank robber in New Haven, Connecticut, was convicted and sentenced to 80 years in prison. His bank robbery was foiled when his getaway car, left idling outside the bank, was stolen.

Police in Radnor, Pennsylvania, interrogated a suspect by placing a metal colander on his head and connecting it with metal wires to a photocopy machine. The message, "he's lying," was placed in the copier and police pressed the copy button each time they believed the suspect wasn't telling the truth. Believing that the "lie detector" was working, the suspect confessed.

■

A would-be robber tried to stick up an Oakland bank. The teller gave him a dummy bag with marked bills and an explosive set to detonate at the bank's door. He stuffed the bag down the front of his trousers, and the device worked.

■

Two suspects, ages 20 and 21, were arrested and charged with stealing a statue of Ronald McDonald from outside a McDonald's restaurant in Canonsburg, Pennsylvania, and holding it for ransom demands of 150 hamburgers, 150 milkshakes and one diet soda to go. A ransom note signed, "The Hamburglar," and delivered to the drive-in window, threatened to melt the clown into ashtrays to be used at a competing restaurant.

■

Burglars, dynamiting the safe of a Midland, Texas, fast-food restaurant, also blew the currency in the safe into tiny particles.

■

When two service-station attendants in Ionia, Michigan, refused to hand over the cash to an intoxicated robber, he threatened to call the police. They still refused so he called the police and was arrested and charged with disorderly conduct.

Wrong Place at the Wrong Time

In 1986 Richmond, Virginia, police said that a vacationing, 44-year-old newspaper deliveryman from Oakland, California, began shooting at the Waheed Zafir family when they told him that he was driving the wrong way on the one-way street in front of their house. He drove past as the Zafir family was getting into a Dodge van and one of the children yelled at him that he was going in the wrong direction. He then made a U-turn and fired several shots into the van, wounding the mother and chasing the family into their house.

◼

A 32-year-old suspect wanted by the FBI on charges of murder and assault and for questioning in more than a dozen murders and 50 beatings, was arrested by FBI agents as he jaywalked in front of their car in Oakland, California, in 1987. The agents had his picture on the front seat of their car when he walked past and they recognized him.

◼

Thirty-year-old Paulette Fabre, vacationing at Roque Brune-sur-Argens on the French Riviera, was killed when she was struck in the chest by the rib of a runaway beach umbrella while she lay sunbathing. The umbrella had been picked up and propelled by a gust of wind.

■

A London coroner concluded that it was probably the metal underweaving of 62-year-old Iris Somerville's brassiere which attracted the lightning bolt which struck and killed her as she walked through a London park. A burn mark on her chest matched the pattern of metal reinforcing her bra.

■

In 1986, Refugio Tarin, the driver of a pickup truck, and Jesus Carrasco, one of his passengers, killed each other in a gun battle inside the cab of the truck while Tarin was driving. Manuel Carrasco, a passenger in the truck sitting between the two as they fired their weapons, was wounded in the arm and shoulder. Presidio, Texas, Sheriff Rich Thompson said, "It was just three of them in the pickup and they started arguing. The poor guy in the middle didn't have any place to go." Thompson did not know what started the argument.

■

Thinking he was on an interstate highway, Jack Comiskey, 87, drove his rented car down an airport runway at 50 miles an hour, then went off the end of the runway and over a seawall into Tampa Bay. A group of firefighters training nearby rescued Comiskey and his wife from the water. A plane that had been cleared to land on that runway was warned away at the last minute by the airport control tower supervisor who watched Comiskey's drive down the runway.

■

The windshield of Kitty Wolf's car was shattered by a falling carton of several hundred 1.5-ounce jars of jam and marmalade which dropped from a transcontinental airliner. Regent Air was unable to explain how the two cartons of Dickinson's Fancy Sweet Marmalade fell from one of its planes after takeoff from Newark International Airport. FAA officials later determined that a catering service had left the two cases on the doors of the plane's landing gear, where they were forgotten.

Two hours after a bus traveling from Kansas City to Denver departed, the bus's headlights failed. Passengers were then transferred to a replacement bus which broke down about 200 miles from Kansas City. Robbers, one armed with a shotgun, arrived ten minutes after the driver left to get help and took about $1,000 in cash and jewelry from the passengers. The passengers boarded a new bus later that day which was then delayed in western Kansas by a blizzard. It reached eastern Colorado the next day and was again delayed by bad weather.

In 1987 in Texarkana, a man and a woman, after picking up two hitchhikers, led police on a high-speed chase exceeding 100 miles an hour and ending when the stolen car they were driving left the highway, went down a Texarkana street and crashed in a curve. Police were alerted to the car by complaints that a woman was exposing her buttocks through a car window. The couple were charged with auto theft. The hitchhikers were released without being charged.

Eighty-three-year-old wheelchair-bound Henry Schecker of Miami started out for the local library but wound up in the middle of Interstate 95. "I'm not sure how I got there," he told police. "I was going along, and the first thing I knew, I was sitting on I-95."

Thirty-year-old Douglas Hicks of Ashland, Kentucky, was asleep inside a dumpster behind a building in Charleston, West Virginia, when the dumpster was emptied into a garbage truck. A hospital security guard heard Hicks screaming from the garbage truck as it passed by the hospital. The guard chased the truck in his car to alert the truck's driver before the crushing device was activated.

■

Stephanie Taylor was driving on U.S. 79 in northeastern Tennessee when she struck a deer. The deer crashed through the windshield and landed next to her in the passenger's seat. Mrs. Taylor stopped the car, got out and ran away as the animal tried to get out of the car. "When I looked around the deer was gone," she said.

■

Irish steelworker Bob Finnegan was crossing a Belfast street when a taxi hit him. As he lay in the road, another car ran into him, knocking him into the gutter. As bystanders gathered, a small van plowed into the crowd, injuring three people and hitting Finnegan again. When a fourth vehicle headed toward the crowd, they saw it in time and scattered. Only one person was hit—Finnegan.

Reasons Not to Dial 911

When an off-duty Detroit police officer shot himself in the shoulder as he tried to kill a rat that had jumped onto his arm in his garage, ten Detroit police patrol cars responded to the report of a shooting at the man's house. The rat escaped unharmed.

■

An ambulance responding to a call in Odell, Illinois, skidded on snow-covered pavement and ran over James Ritchie, the person the ambulance had been sent to aid. Ritchie, who had been lying on a rural road, may also have been hit by a truck that was following the ambulance.

■

A city ambulance crew in St. Louis in 1980 stopped to pick up a pizza while on their way to the hospital with a patient suffering from head injuries. The ambulance circled the pizza parlor parking lot for about five minutes until the crew's pizza was ready.

■

The police chief of a West Virginia town responded to a report of a man wandering through traffic on a four-lane highway and accidentally struck and killed the man.

■

In 1987, a California sheriff faced criticism for his practices of using chains and handcuffs for female defendants in courtrooms but not using the restraints for male defendants.

■

One guest drowned at a 1985 pool-party attended by about 100 New Orleans lifeguards who were celebrating their first drowning-free season in memory. At the end of the party the body of Jerome Moody was found fully clothed at the bottom of the deep end of the pool.

■

In Long Beach, California, in 1984, a meter monitor ticketed an illegally parked car, thinking that the murder-suicide victims in the front seat were asleep. The two victims were discovered hours later, dead of gunshot wounds to their chests. "She's not a police officer and you can't expect her to act like one," said a homicide detective.

■

Police in San Diego, California, abandoned their restraint policy after an uproar over an incident in which a mounted police officer led a black man through neighborhood streets by a rope attached to the horse's saddle. The man had been arrested for walking a dog without a leash.

■

A sheriff's deputy in Joliet, Illinois, responding to an accident in which a car plunged into an unmarked construction pit, accidentally drove his own patrol car into the pit, landing on top of the accident victim's car and crushing her to death.

■

Three firefighters on their way to a fire in East Windsor, New Jersey, had to be treated for inhalation of toxic fumes when a fire broke out on board their fire truck and ignited the hoses.

A 19-year-old woman was rescued from the Atlantic Ocean by police in Long Beach, New York, after failing to prove that she could swim while wearing handcuffs. The woman, who had been pounded against the rocks by the waves, was arrested and charged with disorderly conduct.

A jail guard in White Plains, New York, trapped during a prison riot in 1981, tried several times to call county police collect but had difficulty getting them to accept the charges.

Firefighters in Thurston County, Washington, slept while their station burned. The station had been burning unnoticed for at least one hour before a passing police officer turned in the alarm.

In Avellino, Italy, Carmine Urciuolo was riding unattended in the back of an ambulance after it picked him up at a traffic accident. He slid out the unfastened rear door and had to hitch-hike to the hospital.

In 1986 a woman was freed from a pair of designer jeans by San Jose, California, firefighters who worked for twenty minutes using wire cutters and needle-nosed pliers.

Famous Collectors

After Clint Bolin vacated his Long Beach, California, apartment, his landlord discovered 600 boxes containing 30 tons of assorted rocks, chunks of concrete and slabs of cement stacked to the ceiling in every room. Bolin left only a narrow channel connecting a couch, where he presumably slept, and the toilet. Nearby motel owners claim Bolin left rocks at their establishments as well, averaging several hundred pounds per overnight visit.

■

A St. Petersburg, Florida, man was arrested and charged with taking at least 370 dirty diapers from people's front porches while posing as a diaper service driver. Police, who couldn't discuss a possible motive for the alleged thefts, said that the diapers were found cleaned and folded in a closet in his home. The suspect, who has no children, said that he neither sold nor loaned any of the diapers. However, he was wearing a disposable diaper when he was arrested. At least 1,500 diapers had been reported missing in the area.

■

When 52-year-old Patricia Wittlesey of Santa Monica, California, became ill and was hospitalized, animal control agents found 70 live cats and the bodies of about 100 dead cats in her home. The dead cats were wrapped in plastic and stacked in cardboard boxes up to the ceiling, many labeled by name and time of death. "Dawn, born April 17, 1970 died Saturday 2 A.M. Feb. 2, 1976 of my breeding her to Chowder," read one box. Another read, "Bunny by Vandle. Most beautiful tart. Killed her."

■

A 34-year-old Yukon, Oklahoma, man was charged with unlawfully obtaining charitable donations after he said that he posed as a doctor to collect breast milk from unsuspecting mothers.

■

The Louisiana Department of Correction's internal affairs division said that prisoners have been systematically swindling unsuspecting pen pals out of money and other items. One common scam threatens female correspondents with the death of an inmate unless they mail nude photos of themselves to the prison. One inmate was found to have a collection of 600 photos of nude women of all ages.

■

Firefighters and sanitation workers in San Jose, California, were called on to remove over 25 tons of garbage stored in a two-bedroom home in 1988. It appears that the residents collected garbage, often rummaging through trash cans and garbage dumps. The couple and their three adult sons also had rented two public storage lockers for overflow garbage and had planned to rent a third. One son said that the mess "was a whirling force that seemed to wheel out of control," but that he was grateful that the secret was out. Firefighters found the house's floor covered with rotting garbage, feces, maggots, and rodents. The first one to open the door reported that he was nearly felled by "a swarm of flies" and mice "by the score."

■

In Peoria, Illinois, a man was fined $500 in 1988 for having tricked 50 women into giving him their underwear for his collection. He had convinced the women by telephone to leave their underwear outside their apartment houses so he could use it to play tricks on their boyfriends. The man said later, "I had no intention of it getting out of hand. It's just something that happened to me recently."

■

A 23-year-old man was arrested and charged with stealing 732 books and 56 record albums from the library of the University of North Carolina at Greensboro. The thefts took place over two years. Police said that the man wanted to add to his collection.

■

Another book collector is Jerry Gustav Hasford, author of the novel *The Short Timers* on which the Vietnam War movie *Full Metal Jacket* was based. Police from the California Polytechnic State University served a search warrant seeking 87 overdue books that had been checked out of the school's library in Hasford's name. They found a pair of storage units rented in the author's name which contained over 10,000 books, belonging to libraries in England and Australia as well as from libraries in Sacramento, California, and St. Louis, Missouri.

Memorable
Joyrides

Two unidentified men took a 112-ton Chicago & North Western locomotive on a 50 mph joyride in 1988. Their ride ended when the engine derailed.

■

In 1987, police from five law enforcement agencies chased a 19-year-old private on a 70-mile joyride he took with a 27-ton Army howitzer tank. Police chased him until he ran out of gas and then arrested him and a civilian, and charged them with stealing the vehicle from Fort Carson.

■

In 1982, Pvt. Charles Keefer, 20, stole a 50-ton M-60 tank from the Army's Sullivan Barracks in Mannheim, West Germany, and drove it through that city for 2½ hours. As Keefer drove wildly through the narrow city streets, he crushed 14 cars, damaged several shops and houses, tore a 3-foot wide hole in the side of a streetcar filled with passengers and ripped down power lines. Several auto accidents were attributed to Keefer as drivers attempted to get out of his way. Keefer drowned when the tank finally crashed into the Neckar River, landing upside down.

■

A Soviet tank crew on maneuvers in Czechoslovakia in 1984 got lost and traded their tank to a tavern owner for 25 bottles of vodka, 7 pounds of herring and pickles. The tavern owner dismantled the tank and sold the pieces to a metal-recycling center. The soldiers were found asleep in a forest two days later.

∎

A 20-year-old man was arrested in 1986 and charged with stealing a bus and driving it several times from the Port Authority Bus Terminal in Manhattan across the George Washington Bridge to Fort Lee, New Jersey, and back again. He charged passengers 50 cents a trip and collected $88 in fares. "He looked exactly like a bus driver. He had on a shirt and tie and a change thing at his waist," said a Port Authority officer.

∎

A Los Angeles man who said later that he was "tired of walking," stole a steamroller and led police on a 5 mph chase until one officer jumped aboard and brought the vehicle to a stop.

∎

While an ice cream truck driver was making a delivery in Oakland, California, a 33-year-old man hopped into the Carnation Co. truck and took it on a wild ride through busy city streets. The deliveryman hitched a ride to chase the man and watched as the ice cream truck hit five cars, three parking meters, and a building and finally crashed into a telephone pole. "The first words out of his mouth were 'I am on drugs and I am not responsible,' " said motorcycle officer Kevin Taylor.

∎

A 30-year-old East Wenatchee, Washington, man led four patrol cars on a five-hour chase after he drove an eight-wheeled diesel farm tractor with five-feet tall tires away from Loomis Tractor of Waterville, Washington. Two of the officers tried to head him off by parking their patrol cars on either side of an intersection with their lights on to get his attention. The tractor did not stop or drive by but drove directly over both vehicles, crushing the $25,000 patrol cars. He then drove into a wheat field with the remaining patrol cars in pursuit. The tractor was brought to a halt as the officers fired several dozen shots into the tractor body and its tires, so damaging the vehicle that the sheriff's department said that it would have to pay $25,000 to replace the tractor.

■

Two brothers drove a Honda station wagon away from Randy's German Car Repair in Boca Raton, Florida. The brothers, aged 6 and 8, had painted mustaches on to look older. When a police officer blocked their path with his patrol car, the boys put the car into reverse and drove backward across an intersection and crashed into a wall. Police Sgt. Robert Muth noted that they hadn't intended to go in reverse and that they thought they had "put it in 'R' for race."

■

In 1988, a 17-year-old was accused of taking a California Highway Patrol car on a round trip drive from San Francisco to Sacramento. Three years earlier, the same teenager took a joyride in a San Francisco city bus and was wounded by police gunfire after returning the bus and trying to flee. Just five months prior to the patrol car incident, a jury awarded him $150,000, ruling that the officer had used excessive force.

■

An 18-year-old was arrested and charged with the unauthorized use of a vehicle after he apparently took an Army weapons carrier from an Army National Guard Armory in Annapolis, Maryland, and drove it about 50 miles to Washington, D.C. He drove the camouflaged High Mobility Multipurpose Wheeled Vehicle (or "Hummer") through Washington streets as he was chased by several patrol cars. After damaging two police cars, the vehicle slammed into a protective barrier outside the U.S. Capitol.

Mistaken Identities

In 1987, a 61-year-old retired Army sergeant shot a woman he mistook for his estranged wife outside a church in Rochester, New York. "I'm sorry about the other woman," he told police. "I meant to kill my wife, but I forgot my glasses."

■

A Westchester, New York, man shot and killed his wife while hunting, telling police that he had mistaken her for a woodchuck.

■

A man shot and killed his friend Laurel Lange of La Crosse, Wisconsin, while hunting, telling police that he mistook Lange for a squirrel.

■

Hunting near Proctor, West Virginia, in 1988, a man killed Wanda Rogers, 14, when he mistook her for a groundhog.

■

A 33-year-old Virginia Beach, Virginia, man told police that he had mistaken his mother-in-law for a large raccoon when he killed her in his garage with a hatchet in 1981. He said that after he hit her once, he realized it was his mother-in-law and then he hit her again. "I . . . snapped or something," he said.

He was later convicted of second-degree murder. During his trial, his wife testified out of loyalty that she had committed the crime.

■

In Africa in 1987, a driver for a logging company saw Tumago Wonde at work in her garden, mistook her for an evil spirit and hit her on the head several times with a piece of iron. After laying unconscious for an hour, Wonde crawled into her house, summoned aid and was hospitalized.

■

A St. Louis, Missouri, woman killed Joel Robinson by running over his head with her car. She explained to police, who charged her with first-degree murder, that she had mistaken Robinson for her boyfriend, with whom she had quarreled.

■

When the identities of two teenage female victims of a car crash in Decatur, Indiana, were mixed up, the family of the victim who had actually died in the crash granted their permission to end life support efforts for the surviving victim who they had been told was their daughter. The switch was discovered by a family friend who viewed the body at a funeral home.

■

Patrick Sisk of Sisk Brothers funeral homes in Connecticut filed a complaint against the Yale–New Haven Hospital, claiming that the bodies of two men who died on the same day and were both transported to two Sisk Brothers funeral homes had been misidentified. "The tags were wrong," said Sisk. The mix-up led to the body of the wrong man being cremated. The switch became evident as horrified mourners saw the wrong man in the coffin at the funeral-home viewing.

They Still Do That?

In 1987 the Soviet freighter Slutsk was boarded by three pirates armed with knives as it left Singapore bound for Vietnam. The pirates attempted to rob the chief engineer in his cabin but he drove them all overboard.

◼

Ugandan rainmaker Kazaalwa was killed by villagers who blamed him for causing a hailstorm that destroyed their homes. Kazaalwa had threatened to unleash his powers on the village unless the people there showed more generosity toward him. The villagers forced him out into the hailstorm and beat him to death.

◼

At least 20 suspected sorcerers were murdered in the West Bengal State of India in 1987. All of the slain were women suspected of practicing witchcraft.

◼

Close relatives killed 18 elderly people in northern Tanzania in the summer of 1987 because they suspected them of practicing witchcraft.

◼

Three aborigines asked the United Nations Human Rights Commission in 1980 to condemn oil drilling by the Amax Petroleum Australia Company at the sacred site of their tribe's lizard god, Goanna. The tribe believes that Goanna lives beneath Pea Hill, and that, if disturbed, he will tell the six-foot monitor lizard, the tribe's food source, not to mate.

■

Seventy-four-year-old Pavel Navrotsky, a Soviet military deserter during World War II, was discovered in 1985 after living in hiding for 41 years in a pigsty. During the 41 years, Navrotsky only went out for a walk once, at night, dressed as a woman.

■

In February 1986 the Chinese Public Security Ministry called for strict enforcement of the bans on superstitious practices, saying, "We must crack down with determination on witches, sorcerers and other criminal elements who practice feudal superstition to engage in hooliganism, swindling and even go so far as to kill people." In 1985, a young woman was battered to death in the Chinese province of Guangdong because she was supposedly possessed by a fox spirit that was blamed for damaging young men's sexual abilities.

■

John Kimutai Korir, leader of a sect called the Church of God in Kenya, was convicted of killing a 17-year-old girl during an exorcism. According to the state counsel at his trial, Korir cut open the girl's chest, removed her lungs, placed them in her mouth and then left to pray for the girl. Korir claimed that this action would chase evil spirits from her body.

■

In 1985, China announced that foreigners would be banned from viewing Tibetan sky burials, a practice involving the ritual cutting up of a corpse into small pieces, the smashing of its bones and the feeding of the remains to vultures. The ritual is the most common form of discarding a dead body in Tibet.

Chinese authorities said in a statement that "tourists have gone to these sites without permission, greatly to the distress of the families of the deceased." The announcement also banned the hunting of vultures.

■

In Liberia, six men were sentenced to hang for the killings of two small boys in a ritual intended to influence voters in a mayoral election. The mayoral candidate, mortician Joshua Bedell, enlisted the aid of former judge Alfred T. Davies who masterminded the kidnaping and murder of the 6- and 7-year-old boys in order to remove two left eyelids and a penis for the ritual. All of those involved in the crime had higher political ambition as motives for their participation. Davies admitted that he got involved because "I wanted to be a consultant."

Feuds

Charlene and Gerald Tymony, who are black, believe their neighbor Sue Kaufman deliberately trained her parrot to say "nigger" because the Tymonys would not trim their trees to improve Kaufman's view from her Seattle hilltop home.

■

Police charged a Waynesburg, Pennsylvania, physician with kidnaping his former stockbroker from his firm's Christmas party in 1983. Dressed as Santa Claus, he abducted the stockbroker from the party and held him in a shed for 12 days where he tortured him with cattle prods and a homemade electric chair, punched him, injected him with an unknown substance, and sprayed him with mace. Police said that the man was upset over trading losses amounting to $300,000.

■

An old-style feud between the Johnson and Collins families flared up again in Grand Ridge, Florida, in 1988, when someone's car lights shone annoyingly into one family's house. An ensuing gunfight left three dead and three wounded.

■

A 20-year family feud in Taipei between the Yuehs and the Taos, which began when the families owned competing billiard halls, erupted when Mr. Yueh was killed for spitting at the

Taos' doorway—which Mrs. Yueh said was in retaliation for the "bad luck" brought to their soon-to-wed daughter by the Taos' spitting at the Yuehs' doorway.

■

A man in Brightwood, Ohio, reported his neighbor dead after the neighbor failed to move from his couch despite the man's repeated knocking at his door. The police investigated but found nothing wrong with the neighbor, who told them he deliberately ignored the knocking. "I have a cold six-pack of beer in my refrigerator," he explained, "and he knows it."

■

Landlord Ugo Putti invited all the tenants of his building in Naples, Italy, to a picnic in the country. When they returned home, they found their building had been demolished. "I do not regret my action," Putti said. "I hated my tenants, and they hated me."

Contests

Nightclub bouncer Paul Kelly won Sydney, Australia's first annual dwarf-throwing contest by tossing 4-foot-tall Bobbie Randell over 9 feet onto mattresses.

■

Death-row inmates at Huntsville, Texas, prison awarded a $280 pot in commissary privileges to the one who picked the minute inmate James David Autry would be pronounced dead. If Autry had won a stay of execution, he would have won the pot.

■

The winning entry (among 500) in the Army Materiel Command contest to name its new national headquarters building (and a $100 prize) was "The AMC Building."

■

Clarence Kinder, a 77-year-old lottery winner in Charleston, West Virginia, won $50,000 in the state lottery in 1987 and died the next day of a heart attack. "(The day he won) was the greatest day of his life," said his stepdaughter.

■

Carl Phillips, one of 10 winners of a 1958 essay contest sponsored by Louisville, Kentucky, radio station WKAY, had to wait 29 years, until March, 1987, for the contest's scheduled pay-off date to arrive. And then he failed to receive the prize promised by the station—an all-expenses-paid trip to the moon. The radio station, which had heard from several other moon-flight ticket holders, told the winners that it was a promotion sponsored by previous owners.

■

On a February day in 1988 more than 200 youngsters in Athol, Massachusetts, searched the snow-covered Kennebunk Woods for two hidden hatchets. The 66th annual Washington's Birthday hatchet hunt was held to remind children of George Washington's honesty.

■

About 20 college teams in the United States annually compete against each other in meat-judging contests. Teams wear color-coded helmets and clothes, and white butchers' aprons. The teams meet in meat coolers in huge privately owned slaughterhouses and judge cuts of meat according to U.S. Department of Agriculture specifications. A six-member panel of judges then picks the winning team.

■

U.S. Marine Corporal Richard Drown died after choking on glazed doughnuts at a speed-eating contest in Newport, North Carolina. Drown had first eaten four doughnuts then two more and stuffed three into his mouth while still swallowing those because he had heard an announcement that only 10 seconds remained in the contest.

Fetishes

Psychiatric counseling was ordered for a 38-year-old Catonsville, Maryland, man after he pleaded guilty to possession of child pornography; a search of his apartment revealed that he slept in an excrement-soiled twin bed made up to resemble a crib, filled with diapers, baby bottles and pacifiers.

■

A student working in the steam room at Central Michigan University uncovered in a locker 1,117 pairs of women's underpants, 79 brassieres and two pairs of women's gym shorts.

■

Police in Clarkstown, New York, searched for a man wearing a large white diaper who was approaching children near school bus stops and asking, "Where's the masquerade party?" "We want to talk to him," said a police official.

■

In 1987 police arrested a 26-year-old sheet metal mechanic from Quartz Hill, California, for allegedly sucking the toes of a maternity store clerk. The 20-year-old woman said that the man claimed to be a podiatry student. Police were later contacted by many women claiming that he used the same story when he approached them in shoe stores, shopping centers and supermarkets. He allegedly offered to show the women how their feet worked before he would suck their toes.

■

Postal authorities accused a former employee of the San Antonio Zoo of having had sex with cats, dogs, horses, ponies, goats, sheep, cows, a pig, a duck, a gazelle, a baboon that had just given birth, and an oryx. Authorities allegedly have incriminating photographs of the 27-year-old man. He told an informant that he wanted a job at Sea World so he could try to have sex with a dolphin.

■

In Houston, a 24-year-old man received only a 30-day jail sentence in 1988, for stealing a $195,000 Trailways bus after he promised to stay away from buses. He estimates that he has stolen at least 100 buses since 1986 because of a 13-year fixation he says he developed when his mother dated a bus driver, who let the boy ride with him "for hours and hours."

Compulsive Behavior

A judge in London, England, granted a divorce to a woman whose husband, a paper cutter, refused to bathe more than once a week, never changed his clothes, and habitually came home from work with his ears stuffed with shredded paper.

■

A 31-year-old Nashville man was arrested more than 40 times during a period of 17 years from 1967 to 1983 for stomping women's feet on the street. He spent at least 11 of those 17 years in jail for footstomping. "The only thing I ever get out of this is jail," he lamented. In 1983, another man was arrested for a footstomping incident in New Orleans. Police said that he was possibly a copycat footstomper.

■

Patrick McCarthy, in his mid-60s, was arrested in New York City for trashing a window in the U.S. Courthouse. It was the 18th time in 20 years that he had hurled a rock through a federal building window. One of his former prosecutors commented, "Really, he's an institution."

■

New York City police arrested a 42-year-old IRS examiner and father of two for being the "phantom spanker" who had lured at least 200 starlets into a Manhattan studio, where he put them across his knee and (with a camera on) spanked them, promising a movie career if they could give him the "perfect scream." His wife was so distraught at the discovery that she refused to post bail.

■

Dr. Ibrahim Shademan performed surgery on a 20-year-old woman to remove a 4.4-pound hairball from her stomach because it was endangering her pregnancy. The woman had chewed her hair since she was a child.

■

By June 1984, Alice Richie of Richmond, California, had been watering her lawn 24 hours a day, every day, for more than a year. Her neighbors took her to court as their lawns turned into swamps. Despite a judge's order to stop and utility bills of $300 a month, Richie continued to water and would not say why.

■

A court in Anahuac, Texas, sentenced a 60-year-old man to five years in prison and a $500 fine for being intoxicated during an accident involving 25 vehicles that killed five people. The man, who had 18 previous drunken driving convictions, pleaded no contest.

■

Interviewed in 1983, a Laurel Springs, North Carolina, man said that he went to bed in 1932 at the age of 16, hadn't sat upright since 1942 and hadn't rolled over since 1960. Although he claims to have fallen ill while a teenager with a sickness that has left him continually exhausted, his postman theorizes that his domineering mother sent him to bed for drinking whiskey and that he became ill from lying there for so long.

■

In 1983, 85-year-old Gertrude Jamieson of Chattanooga, Tennessee, was apparently violating a court order and continuing her 46-year-long harassment of Douglas Thompson by calling him on the telephone, sometimes as many as eight or more times a day. The grudge stems from an incident in 1937 when Thompson, then a 17-year-old paperboy, was bitten by Jamieson's dog and reported it to the Humane Society. The dog was picked up and returned days later. Despite numerous court orders, a stroke, confinement to a nursing home, four months at a penal farm and a judge's order to put a lock on her phone, Jamieson has continued to call. "If she sees a pay phone somewhere, she'll grab it," said Thompson.

■

In Gretna, Louisiana, an 18-year-old woman already charged with harassing her ex-boyfriend by telephoning him 377 times and hanging up, was charged with 48 more counts.

■

A 37-year-old man was booked on a charge of loitering around a public restroom after park rangers found him hiding under a women's outhouse in Montana de Oro State Park in Morro Bay, California. He was reportedly dressed in protective plastic clothing and wearing surgical gloves when he was found sitting on crates amidst the waste. "This guy was like waist-deep," said a ranger. Officials said that he apparently entered the outhouse before dawn and was prepared to stay there the whole day. Rangers hosed him down and took him to jail.

Nude Behavior

A man was convicted in Tifton, Georgia, of slinging lard at women while driving around nude.

■

Some residents in Goleta, California, witnessed a man walk past their home naked from the waist down except for clear plastic wrapped around his genitals and buttocks. One witness followed the man until he went through a hole in a fence and disappeared.

■

In 1982, a 29-year-old man was arrested after crashing his Volkswagen into a White House gate after Washington, D.C., police chased his car for several blocks for speeding. When he crashed, he jumped out of his car naked and ran onto Pennsylvania Ave., where Secret Service agents wrestled him to the ground.

■

A nude, 27-year-old Landover, Maryland, resident was arrested for dribbling a basketball along a highway. When police approached, he jumped down 30 feet from an overpass and onto another highway, where he began to run through traffic until he was finally apprehended.

An unidentified naked man picked up 4-year-old Phillip Briggs in College Station, Texas, tossed him into the air and let him drop to the ground. The man said, "All babies come from heaven" as he tossed Briggs. The man then walked to a liquor store and got dressed in clothes hidden by the side of the store.

■

Edward Jalbert, 25, was struck from behind and killed by a United Airlines plane as it landed at Cox Municipal Airport. Jalbert had been walking naked down the middle of the runway at the time.

■

In 1986 an unidentified man in Pembroke Pines, Florida, was stalking the neighborhood wearing only sneakers and a paper bag over his head.

■

An unidentified nude man at Hawaii's Diamond Head crater was throwing large rocks at tourists and jumping on cars. A guard struggled with him and was shot with his own gun. A Federal Aviation Administration guard then arrived and shot the nude man twice, fatally wounding him.

■

A 32-year-old Lansing, Michigan, man was ordered to undergo psychiatric tests after locking himself in the bathroom of a Piedmont Airlines jet, undressing and trying to flush his clothes down the toilet and running naked down the aisle of the cabin.

■

A 30-year-old Denver man entered a couple's apartment at 2 A.M., took off his clothes and got into their water bed with them. The couple called police who arrived to find the intruder still sleeping on the bed.

■

In 1987, a Rockford, Illinois, police officer pleaded innocent to charges of public indecency for playing six holes of golf while wearing only a shirt and golf shoes.

■

A 19-year-old man robbed five gas stations in London while wearing only a pair of his mother's tights over his face. He said that he didn't want to be identified by his clothes. Witnesses identified him by vaccination marks, skin blemishes and the shape of his body.

■

Marley Shaffer of Deerwood, Minnesota, was chased in her car by a nude man driving a yellow Ford Torino at speeds of over 80 mph. Shaffer said that when the man eventually passed her, she thought the chase was over only to drive over a hill and find him standing in the middle of the road waving his arms. The temperature was 15 degrees below zero. The man got back in his car and continued the chase. When Shaffer pulled into a driveway, the nude man backed his car into the same driveway and fell asleep.

Most Compelling Explanations

In Bransford, Ontario, a carpet shampooer defended an arrest for exhibitionism by claiming that the shampooing machine broke loose, hit him in the groin, and unzipped his zipper.

◼

In Cumberland County, California, a jury acquitted Rev. Andrew M. Buehl of soliciting a prostitute. He explained he thought "oral action" meant that he wanted to "talk" to her because he thought she was ill. TV newsman Marty Bass of Baltimore was acquitted of a similar charge. He claimed that he understood "wanted head" to mean that he wanted "to get inside her head" and do a news story about prostitution in the city.

◼

In 1983, lawyer Leonard Jaques missed a court date and was sentenced by a judge for contempt of court. At a hearing, he explained that he "had the screaming itches of the crotch. I wasn't here because I would have been scratching my testicles constantly." The judge doubled the fine for such a "degrading" explanation.

◼

A Pittsburgh man on why he was apparently throwing rocks at his wife, who was struggling not to drown in the Kanawha River: "I was trying to drive her back to shore."

A Reading, Pennsylvania, jury failed to be swayed by the story of a 37-year-old that he was growing marijuana just to cure his hemorrhoids.

■

The Tennessee Supreme Court ruled in 1985 that just because a man who claims to be Prince Mongo from another planet arrived in court wearing a fur loincloth, goggles and bone beads, that was no reason to jail him for contempt. Mongo said that his "spiritual attire" was part of his religious practice.

■

In 1988, a woman in Alaska took a police car that had been left running unattended and proceeded to crash it into a nearby building. She told police that she took the car because she had to go to California.

■

Miami police said that Rosendo Saavedra was killed when he "suddenly jerked backwards and hit his head on the end of the . . . shotgun" being held by the officer searching him.

■

Cheung Yun-fuk, 33, of Hong Kong, said that he has been unable to control his right thumb since his childhood and told a court that it was to blame for pinching a woman's bottom as he helped her out of a taxi.

■

Pregnant Susan Ann Yasger convinced a judge in Orange County, California, that her fetus qualified as a passenger in her car and therefore she was not driving alone on a freeway lane reserved for cars carrying more than one person.

In 1987 psychiatrists testified that Randall Husar, the man who used a hammer to smash the glass cases containing the United States Constitution and the Bill of Rights in Washington, D.C., believes that "Republicans have a conspiracy against him and that they are broadcasting messages to him (through automobile radios)." One psychiatrist who urged that Husar be transferred from Washington to an institution in his home state of Colorado, said, "His continued close approximation to all things Republican does not serve society well here. In a city that lives and breathes politics, the Republican administration continues to remind him of the seed of his delusion."

Happenings in the Home

A Holland, Massachusetts, couple were held for psychiatric observation when police discovered 87 dogs and 35 cats in their trailer, which was three feet deep with excrement. Said Clarence Rogers, 69, "I admit it was bad judgment, but I had to put (the animals) somewhere."

■

A house burglar in Logan, Oregon, known as "The Muncher," has broken into rural homes to eat food, drink beer, watch TV and then clean up after himself. Local sheriffs believe that a copycat "Muncher" may also be at work.

■

Frazer Pahlke sold his family's 9-room house without his wife's knowledge while she and their four children were at an amusement park. When he picked them up at the park, he drove them to a different house and said, "This is where we're going to live." Pahlke said that he sold the home to divest himself of as much property as possible so that he wouldn't have to divide any with his wife when he divorces her.

■

Thieves in Des Moines, Iowa, stole the siding from Glen Taylor's home while he was at a funeral. Taylor's wife said that she had seen men removing siding from other homes in the area. Aluminum siding can be sold for 30 or 40 cents a pound.

Thieves across the country, known as "urban miners," have also been stealing copper pipe and brass fittings from vacant homes.

■

In 1978, a Glenmont, New York, man walked into the home of Mr. and Mrs. Arvid Johnson, took a bottle of wine and one of rum, and went into their bedroom, where he was found on the bed drinking, smoking and reading a book. He refused to leave, telling the Johnsons that it was "my house now." He was once found outside his house with his body wrapped only in aluminum foil, as he explained that a neighbor was beaming gamma rays at him.

■

A Brooksville, Florida, man, angered over his wife's new hairdo, tried to kill her by cutting a hole in their waterbed and holding her head under water. His wife's son stopped him by hitting him with a walking stick. The son said that the man had been waving a pistol around in their mobile home.

■

After resolving a family feud that left members out of communication for years, a brother and sister in Duluth, Minnesota, discovered that neither knew the whereabouts of their 80-year-old mother. Realizing that neither had been caring for her, they went to her home and found that her body had been decomposing for a year. "It sounds dumb, but that's what happened," said a son-in-law.

■

In 1985 Robert Latta, a vacationing Denver water meter reader, wandered into the White House on the day of President Reagan's swearing in. Latta mingled with 33 members of the U.S. Marine Orchestra and entered the White House with them. When he returned to Washington months later

for a court hearing on a charge of unlawful entry, Latta
was seen in the Senate Gallery where he asked to be allowed
to speak on the floor of the Senate.

■

Mr. and Mrs. Joseph A. Carlone had tried unsuccessfully to
rid their Ohio home of a noxious odor since 1964, but it wasn't
until 1972 that the forty gallons of human excrement that had
been accumulating behind their kitchen wall exploded into their
house. Apparently a telephone installer in 1964 had accidentally drilled through a waste pipe leading from the upstairs bathroom, allowing the excrement to fall from the pipe into the wall.

Government in Action

The U.S. Postal Service ruled that a Johnsonville, North Carolina, postmaster had to repay $44 in stamps and money orders that thieves made off with after he told them how to open a Postal Service safe at his grocery store. Four gunmen had pistol-whipped him, threatened him, his wife and eight others and shot his son. The Postal Service said that he failed to "exercise reasonable care."

■

In Jerusalem, several legislators brawled in the Knesset dining room over the lack of hospitality being shown a visiting Soviet peace delegation (whose members were watching).

■

The Army Corps of Engineers inadvertently bulldozed half of an 8-square-mile archaeological site in Delaware containing fossils 80 million years old.

■

The U.S. House of Representatives Gym Committee voted to close the House gym between 10 P.M. and 6 A.M. because Rep. Richard K. Armey (R-Texas) was using one of the changing cubicles as his primary Washington residence.

Four hundred thirty-one Air National Guardsmen were flown to a Nashville bowling tournament in May 1980 at taxpayers' expense of $110,000.

■

In 1987, Chicago alderman Lawrence Bloom gave up on his idea of tattooing pit bulls on the inside lower lip to identify them because he could find no one to volunteer to do the tattooing.

■

The Virginia Corrections Department decided to air condition the death chamber at the State Penitentiary to make it "more comfortable for everybody."

■

The California Division of Industrial Safety has banned weed-pulling and crop-thinning by hand because it causes back injuries. The DIS recommended the use of long-handled hoes instead.

■

Saudi Arabia imported five tons of sand from a Dutch company in 1979 for use in filtering swimming pool water—a job for which Saudi Arabian sand is unusable.

■

Illinois Governor James Thompson cancelled a performance of "The Condom Rag," a song performed once under the auspices of the state's Public Health Department that was to be part of a state-sponsored campaign promoting safe sex. Song lyrics included, "And remember boys, don't be no dunce, only use that condom once," and "Pardon the pun, it's in the bag. All you gotta do is the condom rag."

In 1974 the Consumer Product Safety Commission was forced to recall 80,000 buttons it had distributed to promote toy safety because they were found to be a danger to children. The buttons, which said, "for kid's sake think toy safety," used a paint with dangerously high lead content, had sharp edges and parts that could be swallowed by a child.

A 19-year-old was twice rebuffed by Texas prison officials when he tried to turn himself in in an aggravated assault case. He was turned away one day because he hadn't made an appointment and on another day because he had arrived too late. He was eventually sentenced to a two-year prison term.

The Internal Revenue Service penalized George Wittmeier $159.78 for not paying all his tax with his return. Wittmeier underpaid by a penny.

In the Prince George's County, Maryland, "escape-proof" correctional center's first year of operation, thirteen prisoners were mistakenly released because of human or computer error.

Unexplained Phenomena

In 1979, three elderly Cincinnati women, who had each been married to the same man at different times during the past six decades, all died within 24 hours of each other. The former wives died in reverse order of their marriages.

■

Ninety-two minutes after Michael Stott, 16, of Canandaigua, New York, collapsed and died while watching television at a friend's house, his brother, Christopher, 10, also collapsed and died. Seven years earlier, a cousin to the boys also died suddenly. Doctors suggest a congenital heart defect may have been to blame in all three cases.

■

Geologists from the Interior Department reported that a giant chunk of earth 10 feet long, 7 feet wide and weighing several tons was uprooted from a wheat field in Grand Coulee, Washington, and deposited upside down 73 feet away. Scientists said that there was no evidence of machinery in the area and that it looked like "a giant cookie cutter" had been used.

■

Faye Knowles, driving with her family through the Australian outback in 1988, said that a UFO levitated their car, covered it with dust and threw it back to earth. She also said that throughout the phenomenon, her speech and that of her sons were distorted. Police report that shortly after the Knowles incident, they received a report from a tuna boat crew 50 miles away that a UFO buzzed them and that during the incident the voices of the crew became unintelligible. Police said that the crew could not have known about the Knowles sighting.

■

According to the March, 1988, issue of the *Archives of Surgery*, researchers who examined the medical literature for the history of things people have swallowed found only 31 cases of toothbrush swallowing. Of those 31 cases, 4 occurred in Durham, North Carolina, in 1986.

■

A female monkey in the city of Kanpur, India, jumped onto a high-tension wire and electrocuted herself, causing a blackout of the city lasting several hours. Ten days earlier, her mate had died when he jumped onto the same wire and also caused a blackout. The United News of India reported that the female monkey visited the site of her mate's death daily until jumping herself.

■

A New London, New York, couple were forced to flee their house in the summer of 1988 after more than 2,000 bats moved in. A state department of health bat specialist said that the couple's home had become a "maternity colony" consisting of female little brown bats. At one point so many bats got into the rooms of the house that the husband began to kill them with a tennis racket. "He got 11 of them," his wife said. "He has a wicked backhand."

■

Five people have disappeared in Winyah Bay near Georgetown, South Carolina, since 1977, all on Feb. 13. Two men disappeared in their 10-foot outboard on Feb. 13, 1977, only to be found dead near Charleston days later. Two others disappeared on Feb. 13, 1982, after setting out in their 18-foot boat. Both bodies were again found near Charleston many days later. On Feb 13, 1988, the fifth man fell off a boat ladder and disappeared into the waters of the bay.

Uncategorically Weird

A convicted killer in Florida spent seven years in prison in a wheelchair convincing authorities he was a paraplegic. One day he jumped from his wheelchair onto a startled guard, grabbed the officer's gun, then took the guard, a medical technician and another inmate hostage. He exchanged clothes with the guard and forced the other prisoner to drive the four of them to Fort Myers.

There they got into a minor traffic accident. When he got out of the car to inspect the damage, the hostages drove off and left him standing there. He then persuaded the driver of the other car to take him to a store. When the driver got out, he stole the car.

■

In 1987, players for the Stroitel Cheropovets soccer club in the Soviet Union denounced their manager for corruption. They accused him of keeping the money that they had given him to bribe referees.

■

Two police officers in Lynn, Massachusetts, tried to arrest the owner of a pit bull terrier on a robbery charge. During the struggle, the man, Lugene Kendricks, bit patrolman William Althen on the arm and Edward Kiley on the hand. The dog just watched.

■

The parents of the first child born by artificial insemination through the "Nobel sperm bank" had previously lost custody of two other children after abusing them to make them smart. The two children said their natural mother and stepfather gave them extra schoolwork to do at home and that their stepfather whipped them with straps when they made mistakes. The couple also served prison sentences for fraud three years before the 1982 birth of Victoria, fathered anonymously by a contributor to the sperm bank in Del Mar, California, which collects sperm from Nobel Prize winners and other "creative, intelligent people" to inseminate women who hope to produce geniuses.

■

A Polish railroad worker visiting the French Riviera missed his train while mailing some letters. He then boarded two wrong trains before ending up in the frontier town of Strasbourg. There he sneaked into a railroad station control center and out of curiosity pulled a switch, accidentally causing a train to derail.

■

From 1974 until his discovery by police in 1982, a man in Wigan, England, hid from the authorities in a 21-inch-wide hole under his living room floor which was covered by a carpet and a sofa. Wanted for an assault charge, he had lost 98 pounds as well as his front teeth and had grown a long beard during his years under the floor. He said that while in hiding he "was thinking of what his wife and the kids were going through. It was terrible lying there listening to them talking and playing but unable to let them know I was there." Over the years he began to come out of his hiding place more often and was introduced to his own children as their mother's friend "Michael."

■

Medical researchers, tabulating cases in which items were recovered from the rectums of patients, reported 700 items from 200 patients, including: a live, shaved, declawed gerbil; a bottle of Mrs. Butterworth's syrup; an ax handle; a 9-inch zucchini; a 14-inch vibrator with two D-cell batteries; a plastic spatula; a 9½-inch water bottle; a Coke bottle; a 3½-inch Japanese float ball; an 11-inch carrot; an antenna rod; a 150-watt light bulb; a screwdriver; four rubber balls; 72 jewelers' saws (all from the same patient, 29 at one time); a paperweight; an apple; an onion; a plastic toothbrush package; a frozen pig's tail (which got stuck after it thawed); a 10-inch length of broomstick; an 18-inch umbrella handle; a banana encased in a condom; two Vaseline jars; a whisky bottle with a cord attached; a teacup; an oil can; a 6-inch by 5-inch tool box weighing 22 ounces; a 6-inch stone weighing two pounds; a baby powder can; a test tube; a ballpoint pen; a peanut butter jar; a flashlight; a turnip; a pair of eyeglasses; a hard-boiled egg; several tumblers and glasses; a file; a polyethylene waste trap from the U-bend of a sink; and a Carborundum grindstone with handle.

■

Police in Crown Point, Indiana, treated the death of James A. Cooley, 52, as a suicide for several weeks until public pressure forced a reopening of the case and its treatment as a homicide. Police acknowledged all along that Cooley died as a result of 32 hammer blows to the head.

■

A 62-year-old man was arrested for disturbing the peace and littering for a 1984 incident in which he began tossing items from his 16th-floor apartment out the window. He started with a mattress, a TV set, and a telephone, followed by cameras, picture albums, food, beer, pots and pans, piles of newspapers and telephone books, "nudie magazines," a set of encyclopedias, mayonnaise jars, two bicycles and six new bicycle tires, and new and used clothing. When someone in the crowd below yelled "Icebox!" he pushed his refrigerator out, followed (at the crowd's behest) by the stove and other large pieces of furniture. His niece told reporters after his arrest that "Everybody has their off days."

■

In 1978 a Stanford student bludgeoned his academic adviser to death with a sledgehammer, blaming him for blocking his progress during his 19-year career in the school's graduate math program. By the time of the murder he had lost his job and his wife and had only $24 to his name. He said that his adviser, Karel deLeeuw, treated him in a condescending manner and teased him for wearing wing-tip shoes. After killing deLeeuw, he spent his remaining cash on a pizza and a beer and then turned himself in. He said that he contemplated murder for quite a few years but that he first finished work on his thesis so that the murder wouldn't look like "sour grapes." Professors who testified at his trial said that his thesis only needed to be typed when the murder took place. "After killing deLeeuw, I got what I wanted," he said. "I have the leisure to study without the distractions of having to support myself. I view prison as a sort of utopia with constraints."

During his time in prison, he refused conditional parole offers three times because he would not agree to stay away from Stanford. Upon his release from prison in 1985, he said, "I have no intention of killing again. On the other hand, I cannot predict the future."

Sources

Agence France-Press

American Medical News

The American Spectator

Anchorage Daily News

The Arizona Republic

The Associated Press

Automotive News

Bangkok Post

The Black Mountain News (Black Mountain, North Carolina)

Boston Herald

California Magazine

The Charlotte Observer

Chicago Tribune

China Post (Taipei)

The Cincinnati Post

The Columbus Dispatch

Constitution (Atlanta)

Daily Express (London)

Daily Press (Newport News, Virginia)

The Dallas Morning News

The Des Moines Register

Detroit Free Press

The Downers Grove Reporter (Downers Grove, Illinois)

The Economist

The Evening News (Harrisburg, Pennsylvania)

The Evening Sun (Baltimore)

Fairbanks Daily News-Miner

Finger Lakes Times (Geneva, New York)

Fortune

Freethought Today

Gannett News Service

The Globe and Mail (Toronto)

Goleta Sun (Goleta, California)

The Hartford Courant

Herald-American (Syracuse)

The Houston Post

The Huntsville Times (Huntsville, Alabama)

The Indianapolis News

International Railway Journal

The Journal (Providence)

The Journal of Commerce

Ketchikan Daily News (Ketchikan, Alaska)

Key West Citizen

Lincoln Journal (Lincoln, Nebraska)

Los Angeles Times

The Miami Herald

Monday Magazine (Victoria, British Columbia)

The Montgomery Journal (Rockville, Maryland)

The Morning News (Wilmington, Delaware)

The National Law Journal

The News & Observer (Raleigh, North Carolina)

Newsweek

New York Daily News

The New Yorker

New York Post

The New York Times

The Olympian (Olympia, Washington)

Parade

Philadelphia Evening Bulletin

The Philadelphia Inquirer

The Pittsburgh Press

The Post-Standard (Syracuse)

Press State Service

The Record (Hackensack, New Jersey)

The Register-Guard (Eugene, Oregon)

Reuters

Richmond Times-Dispatch

St. Louis Post-Dispatch

St. Petersburg Times

San Antonio Express-News

San Francisco Chronicle

San Jose Mercury News

San Luis Obispo County Telegram (San Luis Obispo, California)

Seattle Post-Intelligencer

The Seattle Times

South China Morning Post (Hong Kong)

The Star-Ledger (Newark, New Jersey)

Star Tribune (Minneapolis)

The Sun (Baltimore)

Sun-Times (Chicago)

Surgery

Syracuse Herald-Journal

Tampa Tribune

Times (Florence, Alabama)

The Times (Trenton, New Jersey)

The Times (London)

The Times-Picayune

Times Union (Albany, New York)

The Toronto Star

United Press

United Press International

USA Today

U.S. News and World Report

Variety

The Wall Street Journal

The Washington Post

The Washington Times

The Wichita Eagle

PLUME TICKLES YOUR FUNNYBONE

Buy them at your local

bookstore or use coupon

on next page for ordering.

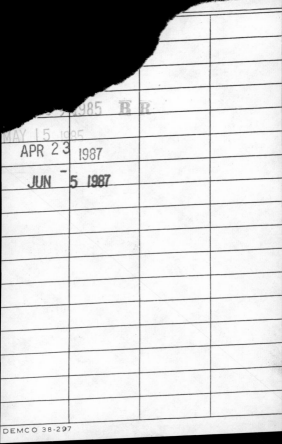